We We[...] D

SELECTED STOR[...] [...]CK HISTORY
IN NORTH KINGSTOWN

G. Timothy Cranston
with Neil Dunay

Other books by G. Timothy Cranston:

Walking in Olde Wickford:
The History of Hamilton Avenue & West Wickford
House at a Time - 2014

Walking in Olde Wickford:
The History of Quality Hill & Talbot's Corner
One Building at a Time - 2012

Walking in Olde Wickford:
The History of Elamsville & the Wickford Business District
One Building at a Time - 2011

Walking in Olde Wickford:
The History of Old Wickford
One House at a Time - 2010

Images of America: North Kingstown 1880-1920 - 2005

Dedication

This book is dedicated to the exceptional works of Mrs. Mel Benson and Mrs. Violet Clark, two North Kingstown School Dept. educators that had an impact in my life as well as countless other young people in our community also to Ace Clark and Stuart Mabray, two wonderful friends who left this world far too early. And finally to my brother and sisters, Kevin, Shelley, and Teattya with love and affection.

Acknowledgements

I'd like to thank the following people who contributed to seeing this important project through to fruition. Thomas Peirce, Darryl Clark, Karen-Lu LaPolice, Valerie Morgan Addison, and Art Hamilton; thanks for your help and friendship. I appreciate the previous work of Maureen Taylor, Walter Schroder, and John F. Capron III and am pleased to recommend their books to all who read this one. The assistance of Civil War expert Robert Grandchamp, Newport Historical Society Librarian Bert Lippincott, and RI State Archivist Kenneth Carlson was invaluable to me, as always they all seemed to know the answer to every question I asked of them. My friend Neil Dunay, whose scholarly efforts are a critical part of this work, was as invaluable as ever; Thanks Neil for all your help and encouragement over the years. I am also very appreciative of the continuing support of HistWick and all of its members. A huge thank you and all my love goes out to my wife Linda, my partner for life, and a person who still has the patience and understanding to put up with my obsessions. And finally to my good friend and graphic designer, Rachel Peirce – Rachel I cannot thank you enough, without your assistance none of this is possible. You all have helped me to bring these people back into the light.

Contents

Preface

TELLING A MORE COMPLETE STORY

For nearly two decades now, I've put some serious time and effort into trying to get an understanding of just what has gone on here in our fair town over the last three and half centuries or so. It's been a journey for me, not only through time, but on a very personal level as well. My ancestors, my kin, were here playing a part in it all, throughout that enormous timeframe. Although I can lay claim to a few important ancestors in my lineage, the vast majority of them have been regular hard working "every man" kind of people just like the thousands upon thousands of other souls who have contributed to the story that is North Kingstown over the centuries. All of them though had a hand, albeit a small one, in shaping this place. That's one of the basic truths I have come to learn – Every person who has lived here has had an impact, has left a mark on time and affected this community. That realization without question has, over time, led me to another truth. This is a truth which carries over into all of New England I believe, and perhaps even farther. You see, what I've found is that much of the source material folks like myself use for research, most of which was written in the Victorian era, as the people of that time began to understand that the past that they knew was being consumed by the break-neck progress of the Industrial Revolution, is written, unintentionally, with a bias that runs clear through it. I'll cut to the chase here. The folks who had both the inclination and the time to write down what they knew about their community's past back there in the 1880s and 1890s were almost to the person, rich white guys. So when you get right down to it, sadly, but again not deliberately, what you have in every local history tome I have ever read, can be summed up like this, "The Story of our Town – As seen, experienced, and recorded by rich white guys." This is a tragedy of sorts because it misses so much; contributions to the community's history by women, by regular everyday folks and yes, by people of color. Black men and women, mixed race folks, men and women who called themselves Native Americans all of these people and the lives they led are silenced by their omission in the story of a community's past.

Once this particular light bulb went off in my head, I decided I ought to do what I can to correct this unfortunate state of affairs, and I have made an effort to focus on those folks whenever I can. We all need to know the story of everyone if we want to truly understand our past. The history of North Kingstown's womenfolk' matters, the history of poor farmers and middleclass shopkeepers makes a difference, and the compelling story of the black men, women, and children who lived here North Kingstown across the centuries is important. We need to tell the story of our town from all of these perspectives. This, in a nutshell, is what this book is all about – an attempt to tell a more complete story.

Introduction

L
ately I've been spending some time pondering the institution of slavery, my ancestor's connection to it, and the part our fair town played in it. I've known for some time that a large portion of my Newport, RI, ancestors owned household slaves. It's easy enough to rationalize it away, to say to yourself, "All wealthy and prominent Rhode Islanders of the 1600 and 1700s owned household slaves. They weren't doing anything wrong in the context of the times." Or, you can rationalize it away by taking into consideration the relative scale of your ancestor's transgressions. "Thomas Jefferson owned a multitude of slaves, and he is considered to be a great man; your relations only had a few, maybe a dozen at the most, so how can they be any worse than a man like Jefferson." But I'm unwilling to let myself off the hook that easily. The fact of the matter is, that the man for whom Cranston, RI, is named after is not better or worse than the man for whom Jefferson, Missouri, has been named after. A slave owner is a slave owner; the scale of the transgression makes no difference. So it's always out there, like the ache you experience from an old injury, it doesn't stop you from living your life, but you feel it just the same.

Our fair town's part in the institution of slavery is a little more complicated, but equally troubling. To start with, as you may or may not know, the colony of Rhode Island and Providence Plantations was the undisputed champion of slaving within colonial America. And although the total numbers pale into insignificance compared to the vast scale of the slaving operations controlled by British and European interests, the hundreds of thousands of souls brought to the New World on Rhode Island owned merchant ships is something that we all must deal with in our own ways. North Kingstown's part in this aspect of slaving is, in turn, insignificant compared with RI's big three of slaving: Bristol, Newport and Warren. There was only one slave trader who called North Kingstown home and his dealings were nothing like the massive operations run by people like the DeWolfe family of Bristol; the undisputed kings of RI slaving. However, Gilbert Updike, of Smith's Castle fame, did turn a pretty penny with his slaving ventures on the 100-ton shop *Mary* captained by George Lawton, He, like all the other RI slavers, loaded up his ship with RI rum purchased and manufactured in Newport, Bristol, Providence, and yes even Wickford, and sent it off to the west coast of Africa where the rum was traded or sold for slaves which would then be loaded on this ship and sailed off to a Caribbean port where the slaves would be sold and molasses would be purchased. The molasses was then brought back to RI where it was made back into rum. This is the basis for the infamous triangle trade of which you may or may not have heard. Each leg of the journey brought an opportunity for profit as slaves, rum, and molasses were traded like the commodities they were at that time. Sort of the colonial and early American version of money laundering and commodity trading all rolled up into one painfully human tragedy.

TRIANGLE TRADE

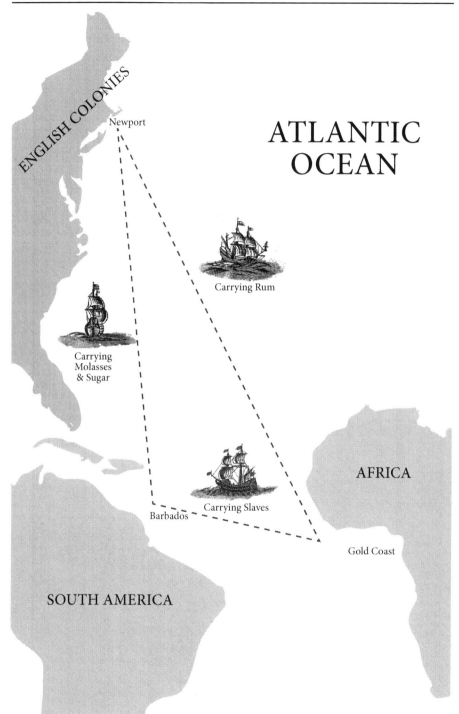

ENGLISH COLONIES

Newport

ATLANTIC OCEAN

Carrying Rum

Carrying Molasses & Sugar

AFRICA

Barbados

Carrying Slaves

Gold Coast

SOUTH AMERICA

A more common North Kingstown connection to this slave trade was the fact that the town was a fairly important source of crew members for the merchant ships involved in this sordid business. A scholarly search of the available crew manifests turns up many names that have a North Kingstown "ring" to them. In a painfully ironic coincidence it has come to my attention that Nathaniel Gardiner, a young man who, until he reached the age of majority, was known around 19th century Wickford as Nathaniel Onion met his end on a ship, which may have been involved in slaving, off the coast of Zanzibar. He was buried at sea and never again saw his sister Thankful Union. I'm sure that the idea of a free black man working on a slaving ship seems as amazing to all of your readers as it did to me when I first thought about it. But it turns out that it was not altogether that uncommon. I guess work was work no matter how distasteful. Whatever the case it was work done for many years by many North Kingstownites, both white and black alike.

All this aside, our town's, as well as our sister community South Kingstown's, greatest connection to the institution of slavery was not made by ships or the men that sailed them or financed them, it was, surprisingly enough made by the countless souls who worked in the fabric mills owned by the scions of the regions, the Hazards and the Rodmans. You see these giants of local industry made their fortunes within a niche of the fabric trade known as Negro Goods. Negro Goods was the general name given to a whole class of fabric made specifically for the southern slave-owning market. The most well-known of these has been given the sanitized name of Negro Cloth and the trade name of Kentucky Jean, but the sad fact of the matter is that it was really known universally at that time, as nigger cloth. I must say that I cringe as I type this even though the word is used in its historical context; it still pains me to concretely acknowledge the facts of the matter. Negro Cloth was made from a combination of hemp (the material used to make twine, rope, and burlap) and coarse cotton or wool. It was the lowest quality material that any mill ever made. It was cheap to produce and had the added benefit of being a profitable place to dispose of all unsuitable yard and mill waste materials. It had to be uncomfortable to wear. It was amazingly profitable and there was a ready market for as much as could be turned out by the mills of southern RI. Other Negro Goods turned out by local mills include: Osnaburg, a coarse cotton wool product one step up from Negro Cloth, Linsey-Woolsey, a linen wool combination which was also of a coarse quality, Nankeen, a slightly better quality plain-woven yellowish cotton cloth named after Nanking Province in China where it was first made, and, the cream of the crop, used for Sunday-go-to-Meeting clothes, calico, a coarse, but printed, all-cotton fabric.

So, you see, the mortar that holds the underpinnings of the villages of Peace Dale and Lafayette together is comprised of Negro Cloth. The same Negro Cloth that was stretched across the backs of countless slaves as they labored endlessly in the fields of the southern United States. It's a fact plain and simple one that we all must confront. Again, it would be easy to rationalize it away. "The Rodmans and the Hazards were just responding to a market need. Negro Cloth is as American as free enterprise and apple pie." But this particular swamp Yankee can't quite swallow that line of logic and I hope the rest of North Kingstown and South Kingstown can't either.

Home & Hearth

THOMAS/WEEDEN/MORGAN HOUSE – 1869

The story of this home, at 115 Pleasant Street, begins with Nancy T. Hazard, who was born on Narragansett Indian tribal lands in 1817. Little can be found about her early life. By the time she was 19, she was raising a young son, named Henry, on her own, and living somewhere in the vicinity of Wickford as she was known to have been employed as a domestic servant for the well-heeled and prominent Hammond family of Wickford and nearby Hammond Hill (the area near the present day intersection of Tower Hill, Shermantown, and Gilbert Stuart Roads). At this same time, she married another member of the Narragansett tribe, a fisherman by trade, Braddock Thomas. The location of Nancy, Braddock, and young Henry's home during this time frame is unknown. One can only imagine what their lives were like. I expect they both worked long, hard hours to make ends meet. Braddock, worked side-by-side with fishing partner Sam Weeden (another Narragansett Indian), harvesting the bounty of Narragansett Bay and Nancy toiled away day after day attending to the needs of the prosperous Hammonds. They don't appear again in the permanent record until the winter of 1858 and, as is often the case, the mark they left is evidence of a great tragedy. The consecutive entries in the town's death register for that time frame tell the tale all too well. First Braddock and then

Sam are listed as "Drown'd in the Narragansett Bay." Nancy and her 19-year-old son Henry were left without a husband and a father. Shortly after this tragic event, Henry married another Narragansett tribal member, Nancy Perry. Henry, it appears, followed in his father's footsteps and became a fisherman. New bride Nancy worked with her mother-in-law as a housekeeper. Somewhere along the line, Nancy Thomas and her son must have made quite an impression upon George Hammond and his bride, a member of a wealthy New York City family, Rebecca Giraud. George and Rebecca, for the most part, lived in New York, but they summered each year in Wickford along with the rest of the large extended Hammond family. I expect, although can not prove with absolute certainty, that George and Rebecca, hired Nancy and her son and daughter-in-law as caretakers for their rarely used Wickford home. This appointment not only guaranteed regular work for the family, but also came with a wonderful bonus. The Hammonds sold a plot of land on Pleasant Street to Nancy Thomas. Rebecca Hammond even held the mortgage for her. So, in January 1869, the land changed hands, the little house was constructed, and Nancy Thomas, a 52 year-old widow, was a homeowner. Even more remarkably, in four short years, the hard working trio paid the note off and owned the place free and clear. Nancy lived out the remainder of her life in her own home, passing on in 1891.

The home was passed on by way of a will, not to Nancy's only son Henry, who was extremely ill by that time with diabetes, but to her 30-year-old granddaughter, Henry's child, Annie Elizabeth, who was married to Thomas Weeden. By this time the era of the Hammonds had passed. Annie Weeden worked as a housekeeper for the Congdon family, who ran the inn known as

Annie Weeden, seated on the right, with her daughter Evelyn (Weeden) Morgan and granddaughter Arlene Morgan.

David W. Morgan (left) and two of his children, Arline and Thomas Morgan (right).

"The Narragansett House" at nearby 71 Main Street. Tom Weeden was a laborer who worked for the state department of roads and highways. When they inherited the house they had a five-year-old daughter, Evelyn. Before long Evelyn joined her mother and worked for the Congdons at their popular inn. Annie Weeden, who was well known and well thought of around town, also worked for a time in the district schoolhouse in the village. She, like her grandmother before her, lived out her life in the little house on Pleasant Street. Upon her death in 1938 at 78 years old, she had lived in the home for 69 years.

The house now passed down to Evelyn who was married to a railroad porter named David Morgan. David worked the trains on the New York to Boston run. Evelyn continued on as a housekeeper even after the Narragansett House closed. They had four children while in the little Pleasant Street home. Sadly, the lure of the big city pulled too strongly upon the railroad porter. He spent less and less time at home with his family until eventually Evelyn divorced him. She took on the monumental task of raising her four children on her own. By all mea-

Thomas Morgan

sures she succeeded in a great fashion. Evelyn lived out her entire eighty years in the little house on Pleasant Street. She joined her ancestors in 1966.

The little cottage now belonged to Evelyn's son Thomas Morgan. He, like all who came before him, lived most of his life within its cozy confines. And he too, added another chapter to the tale of this house. Just as Tom was finishing high school in town, WWII broke out. Tom joined up right away and shipped out before his own graduation. He fought in the war, came back to his hometown of Wickford, worked a long career at Quonset Point in the civil service, and then went to work for Electric Boat. He retired to the little cottage by the bay and lived a quiet but active life full of family and friends.

GEORGE THOMAS HOUSE/OLD YELLOW — 1735

The big house at 6 Bay Street, fondly known for centuries as "Old Yellow" in honor of the milk-based paint it was once white-washed with, has seen more than its share of local history. The building was constructed in 1735 by George Thomas, the first member of that family to settle in the village, and may have originally had some association to the colonial-era shipyard that it was adjacent to. It is the oldest home within the confines of Wickford Village. Over the centuries it has been owned by members of nearly every family that has figured prominently in the history of the community, such as the McSparrens, Mumfords, Slocums, Potters, Northrups, Cottrells, and Bakers; as well as Thomas Cranston and Thomas Brenton, grandsons of two different colonial governors of Rhode Island. In spite of all this history, by far the most interesting period of the house's existence was from about 1885 to 1966 when it was owned by freed slaves Jim and Christina Chase and their descendants. Jim Chase was a Civil War Veteran and respected member of the local Grand Army of the Republic chapter, who was born a slave on a Maryland tobacco plantation, and came here to Wickford after the War with his wife who was also a former slave, and worked as a laborer and a teamster. While in the employ of coal dealer T. S. Baker, Chase purchased "Old Yellow" from his boss and moved in with his family. Eventually, Jim Chase came up with the novel idea of growing, drying, and packaging yeast in the basement of the big house for resale to area bakers and brewers. In this fashion Jim Chase became a respected local businessman as well. Jim and Christina's daughter Mary was born and raised in this house and eventually lived out a long life in Wickford spending much of her time serving as a local midwife, passing on in 1985 her 109th year. By the end of the 20th century, "Old Yellow" had fallen in to a state of severe disrepair and was headed towards possible demolition. A group of concerned Wickford residents banded together, forming a non-profit corporation for the express purpose of acquiring and saving this ancient house. After stabilization of the exterior, the house was sold to and restored by its present owners.

The Chase Family

PECK/FREEBORN HOUSE – 1785

In 1931, the Peck/Freeborn House was sold to Cornelia "Neelie" White. Cornelia White first shows up in the historic record in 1870 as six-year-old Cornelia Parkill under the care of her mother Christiana White who was a live-in domestic servant for James Eldred. At some point between 1870 and 1880 she assumed the last name of White and was living with her mother and her new step-father Jim Chase. Both Jim Chase and his wife Christiana were former slaves and family tradition states that Cornelia's biological father was her mother's former master in Virginia. Cornelia attended school in the village and eventually worked as a domestic servant as well. Jim Chase, a Civil War veteran and coal teamster turned local businessman eventually purchased "Old Yellow," the Bay Street home just behind the Peck/Freeborn House and may have assisted his step-daughter in the purchase of her house in 1931. Just prior to her death in 1954, Neelie White sold the home to her niece Florence (Thomas) Van Hagen and her husband Clarence. Clarence died in 1965 and Florence then lived in the house with her mother Mary Thomas until 1974. When they left the Peck/Freeborn house in 1974 Florence was 79 years-old and her mother was 100. A year or so after moving out Florence passed away. Mary Thomas lived on into her 109th year. She was Rhode Island's oldest citizen when she died.

The little gambrel-roofed home has seen its share of history over the centuries, from sea captains of old to the children of slaves, many different souls have crossed the threshold at 143 Main Street.

Cornelia "Neelie" White, daughter of a former slave, purchased the Peck/Freeborn House in 1931.

DOMINI SMITH HOUSE – 1786

August 19, 1785, must have been a red letter day in the life of local sailor Domini Smith of Wickford. On that day he signed a deed of sale for a house lot on Fowler Street in the village, which he purchased from a prominent local landowner, Samuel Thomas. As Domini was a busy man, sailing on the brig Nancy out of the docks at Wickford on a regular run to the Salt Islands (now known as the Turks and Caicos Islands) with Captain Benjamin Baker at the helm, he most certainly hired someone to build the fine sturdy little Cape Cod-style home for his family. Even though the run to the Salt Islands was fraught with danger — with the British desiring to control the importation of salt into the colonies since before the War of Independence. Smith must have rested a little easier after each watch, knowing his family would soon have a real home and hearth to depend upon while he was at sea. He could do all this for his family because Capt. Baker paid well. Salt was a vital commodity in Wickford, necessary to preserve the massive catch of the village's fishing fleet. This, combined with the danger presented on each run by English warships, meant good, dependable and brave merchant seaman were paid well by Capt. Baker for their skill and service, regardless of skin color. That's right, Domini Smith was former slave Domini Smith, and he worked in the only industry where that fact mattered little. Once the last line was cast off the dock at Wickford, he was just another handpicked member of Captain Benjamin Baker's elite crew, a member of the fraternity of the sea.

Domini Smith, most likely, was connected to either the slave population of the Smith Farm, which was located off of Stony Lane near its intersection with

Post Road, or with the earlier Richard Smith family that settled at Cocumscussoc and were responsible for the Smith's Castle and trading post. Historical records from that family mention a slave named Domini and no other Domini shows up in that timeframe. Beyond these bare facts little is known about Domini's life before 1776 when he first shows up in the historic record as a free man working for Capt. Benjamin Baker on the brig Nancy. As a matter of fact little is known of his life at all. The only fact I know for certain is that he was dead by 1813 as that was the year his son, also named Domini, sold their home to another African-American family, that of William and Robey Clifford. Domini was most likely buried by that same son in the Smith slave burial ground now located deep in the woods in the vicinity of the ancient "Rolling Rock" off of Stony Lane, as those same Smith family records mention a number of African-Americans stopping by the Smith farm long after the days of slavery were over requesting permission to bury a loved one near the graves of their parents and friends. His internment in that slave burial ground marked the end of what must have been an incredible personal journey from a life in bondage to one where Domini Smith was a free man who owned his own home and breathed in the salty sea air of the Atlantic Ocean, a respected member of the crew of the Nancy.

Domini's home was owned by William and Robey Clifford until 1819, when the widow Robey Clifford, listed as a "woman of color" sold the home to Richard Thomas, the son of the man who sold the land to Domini Smith some 34 years earlier.

The "Rolling Rock" located off of Stony Lane.

THOMAS WITHERS HOUSE – 1791

This attractive gambrel-roofed home was constructed by Thomas Withers in 1791 on land he had purchased the year before from Richard Phillips. Nothing is yet known about Withers and his role in the village and by 1793, he had sold his home to Benjamin Fowler. Fowler, who lived elsewhere in the village, held the little house as a rental property that he most likely rented to black mariner Samuel Sambo. Sam Sambo was the son of free black, Job Sambo who, with his wife Deborah and their nine children, farmed land near the North Kingstown — East Greenwich border. Samuel Sambo, who sailed regularly on vessels out of Wickford, purchased the house from Fowler in 1800 with the mortgage being held by Capt. John Peck Case under whom Sambo often sailed. Although exact timeframes are unclear due to poor condition of the early 19th century real estate transaction records, it appears that Samuel Sambo lived in the home for many years, perhaps until the end of his days. Sometime in the 1840s however, ownership of the home was transferred through the Case family to another black mariner, Nathaniel Onion Gardiner in a real estate exchange that went unrecorded at that time.

Nathaniel Gardiner was born Nathaniel Onion, son of Sarah Onion and an unknown father in 1803. Sarah Onion died suddenly and Nathaniel and his sister Thankful became the wards of their Aunt Margaret Onion and her common law husband Richard Gardiner, who was descended from the slaves of Narragansett planter, Ezekial Gardiner. When Nathaniel came of age, he took the last name of his adopted father and began a life as a merchant seaman under the name of Nathaniel Gardiner. Nat Gardiner died at sea onboard the

89-ft. barque *Hector* and was buried at sea in 1851. His family was not notified of his death until years later when the Hector returned to Narragansett Bay. The house and Nathaniel's worldly possessions were left to his sister Thankful Onion, who by that time, was working as a domestic for Allen Mason Thomas. To allow the probate transfer to occur, A.M. Thomas, acting as the agent for the estate of Nat Gardiner, arranged for the official recording of the real estate transaction between the Case family, in the persons of John P. Case's grandchildren Elizabeth Brenton Shaw and John Peck Case Shaw, and Nathaniel Onion Gardiner. This transaction, in which the house was described as the "Sambo place," gave legal ownership of the home to Thankful Onion. Thankful lived in the home until 1870 when she, by then using the new legal name of Thankful Union, sold the home to John P. and Mercy Lewis. Thankful lived out most of the rest of her days in the home of Allen Mason Thomas, spending only her last year at the Town Farm where she died in 1881.

RICHARD THOMAS/JAMES BULLOCK HOUSE 1841/1902

The house that we see today at 101 Pleasant Street consists of a heavily modified small cottage, originally constructed around 1841 for an African-American couple, most probably the children of slaves, Richard and Rachel (Smith) Thomas. Richard Thomas earned his living as a local fish peddler and his wife Rachel, likely related to free black mariner Domini Smith who lived nearby on Fowler Street, worked as a domestic. Richard was most certainly the brother of Nancy Thomas who lived nearby in the still extant Thomas/Weeden/Morgan House. Although none of Richard and Rachel Thomas' children survived childhood it does appear that they raised the orphaned daughter of another African-American neighbor Ellen Berry, as census data shows her living in their home. Rachel died in 1883 and Richard died in 1890. Their home and property were purchased by the neighbor just to the south, master housewright James Bullock.

Heroes & Heroines

THE 14TH RI REGIMENT (COLORED TROOPS) HEAVY ARTILLERY AND THE CEMETERY ON DUTCH ISLAND

In July of 1948, some sixty-four years ago, quietly, somberly, without fanfare or a mention in the local press, a group of soldiers tied up at the long abandoned pier at Fort Greble on Dutch Island and went about their assigned task. They were there to perform a very specific mission, to unearth the remains of 16 soldiers who had died there while constructing some of the island's earliest defenses back at the opening of the Civil War and then carry those earthly remains to the Farmingdale National Veteran's Cemetery on Long Island in New York for reburial. No one was there to mourn these men on that day and few visit their common grave on Long Island today. And that's a shame; for these were indeed special men. These were Black American soldiers, some just freed, some free for generations, who signed up to fight in the great Civil War, they faced both cannonballs of fire and verbal barrages of hatred as members of the 14th RI Regiment, a heavy artillery unit trained to construct, transport, maintain, and fire the massive cannons of the Civil War.

This regiment was formed in August of 1863 under the command of Colonel Nelson Viall, an experienced artillery commander. Its officers were all white men and included Quartermaster Lt. John Peirce of North Kingstown. All of its enlisted men, hundreds strong, from Sergeants on down, were to be men of color, black men and mixed race black/Native Americans one and all. The Providence newspaper at the time commented, "This call excited a lively interest among the colored people of the State." And indeed it did. It also brought interest from the black populace of nearby states as well, and black men came from all over New York and New England to sign up. Sadly racial hatred, although muted by the fact that this large regiment went a long way towards satisfying the RI quota of soldiers demanded by the Federal government, still reared its ugly head and there was considerable grumbling from all-white units about training side by side with the 14th Regiment at the official Dexter Training Grounds in Providence. For this reason, the 14th's training was expedited and actually completed at the location of their first assignment, Dutch Island where they were to begin the construction of Fort Greble.

They arrived on Dutch Island in September of that year and, after hurrying through their remaining training, got to work on the monumental task at hand. The 14th's orders were to construct, arm, and man an eight cannon battery and associated protective earthworks situated such that it would protect the west passage of the Narragansett Bay from any Confederate cruisers and raiders that might come this way. The work was hard, thousands of tons of earth had to be moved to build the fortifications, camps had to set, land had to be cleared, and the accommodations were sparse, tents for the most part, and winter was on its way. Everyone knew death would come a-calling, and it first made itself known on November 7, 1863 when Private Fred Grimes, who came to RI all the way from New York to join up, succumbed to lockjaw which he acquired due to an injury sustained while building the tent city that he and comrades lived in. As winter kicked in, more death followed; men died from tuberculosis, pneumonia, and small pox. By the time spring arrived in 1864, 15 other men had joined Private Grimes in the little graveyard set up on the northeast shoreline of Dutch Island.

Beginning in early 1864 various units of the 14th RI began to ship out to begin work on similar fortifications elsewhere. Cannon batteries were constructed on Matagorda Island, just offshore of Galveston Texas and in the region surrounding New Orleans. By late April of that year, they were all gone from Dutch Island, off to Forts Parapet and Jackson in the insect invested disease ridden Mississippi Delta region to build and man the gun batteries there. Hundreds more RI black men would die in the Delta re-

This photograph of John Sharper, taken at the S.B. Brown studio in Providence, is the only known image of an enlisted man in uniform from the 14th Rhode Island Colored Heavy Artillery Unit. (From Library of Congress, Gladstone Collection of African American Photographs LC-DIG-ppmsca-11176)

gion during the Civil War and they are all buried there at Fort Plaquemine. But that's another story for another time; our tale continues back on Dutch Island with the little cemetery populated by 16 brave black men.

When the men of the 14th Colored Regiment left Dutch Island in the Spring of 1864, the fort was turned over to units made up of older white soldiers who weren't fit for service on the front lines of the Civil War. Of course, no Confederate Raiders ever did come a-calling and it was a quiet easy detail throughout the course of the War. In 1873, at the little cemetery, a seven-foot tall granite obelisk was raised and dedicated in the honor of those 16 men, but beyond that nothing else happened. Fort Greble was active as a shoreline defense position throughout the 19th century and through the time of WWI and then was closed down and abandoned largely. Nothing happened, beyond the passage of time, until that July day in 1948 when the Army came and took those sixteen souls out to a cemetery on Long Island.

Now when I began to look into this tale, I realized that this was a forgotten aspect of our long local story. Few, beyond myself and my friend Walter Schroder, knew anything about these men. No one seemingly even knew their names and that made me sad. When I called the Veteran's Cemetery on Long Island, the gentleman I spoke to, Tony, although he was quite friendly, knew nothing about these men and did not seem too interested in looking anything up for me. When I told him they were mentioned on the Farmingdale Cemetery website he was surprised. That made me sad as well. If nothing else, their names ought not be forgotten and here are the 15 names I know so far:

Private Fred Grimes – NY	Private William Betson – born a slave in MD
Private Dennis Carroll – RI	Private Phillip Cole – RI
Private John Kenney – RI	Private Charles Roberts – RI
Private Aaron Saunders – NJ	Private Benjamin Smith – RI
Private Lemuel Smith – CT	Private James Walker – RI
Sergeant Josiah Walker – RI	Private George Washington – RI
Private Joseph Whitfield – NY	Private Edward Williams – RI
Private George Hatfield – CT	unknown

In 1898, one of those white officers, Lt. William Chenery of Providence, a well-known and accomplished printer, wrote a history of the 14th Rhode Island. It was reprinted in 1969 by the Negro University Press and there are, thanks to the Negro Press, copies available to peruse. Although the description of the 14th RI's exploits in the War are well written and invaluable, Chenery spent more than half of the book detailing the lives of the 30 or 40 white officers and only offered us a simple list of the hundreds of proud and brave black men who served in the regiment. Although, their individual stories are left up to our imaginations, at least now we all know who these 16 fine men were. If any one out there ever goes to the Farmingdale Veterans Cemetery, I sure would appreciate a photograph of the common grave of these men and I'll share it with all I can.

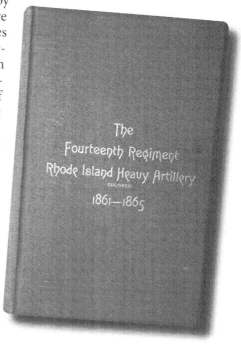

The Fourteenth Regiment Rhode Island Heavy Artillery COLORED 1861–1865

THE CHASE/THOMAS FAMILY

This is a story that's been a long time coming; the telling of a tale that's long overdue. You see, on March 6, 1985, the whole of Rhode Island ought to have held its collective breath for a moment. The little seaside village of Wickford should have observed a moment of silence. The community of souls that makes up our world should have taken notice. For on that day, a woman who was well into her 109th year drew her last breath. A Wickford girl, born of slave parents, who lived out her whole life there, in the village of her birth, was no more. The State of Rhode Island lost its oldest citizen, and its African-American community lost a hero. Mary Thomas, "Old Yellow's" (6 Bay Street, Wickford) long-time resident was dead.

To understand Mary Thomas, it is necessary to take a look at her parents, Jim and Christina Chase, and the life they led before their eventual migration to Wickford. Indeed, in order to fathom Mary's life, you've got to know the story of James Alexander Chase and his bride, Christina White. Theirs is a story worthy of a Hollywood movie or a PBS documentary; it's a tale of determination and perseverance bound up in love of country and each other. It is both unique to them and so typical of the type of experience encountered by countless people in their same situation; slaves who were now free, but not; men and women deservedly ecstatic about their freedom, but with little idea of how they will make it in the rapidly changing world swirling around them.

Jim Chase was born a slave in Prince George's County, Maryland in 1841 of Alexander and Elizabeth Chase. Nothing is known at this time of his early years. He next turns up in the historic record when he, upon his emancipation from slavery, immediately enlists in the 23rd Maryland Regiment, Company F, of the U.S. Colored Troops to fight for his country and the President who had just freed him, through the long bloody Civil War. He served continuously from his initial enlistment until the very end of the war. After the war's end, Jim turns up in New York City, working as a laborer, where he meets his bride-to-be, Christina White.

Christina White was born a slave in Richmond, Virginia in 1843. Even less is known of her early years, other than that she too, migrated to New York City where she met up with Jim Chase. At the time she met her husband-to-be she already had two children; Cornelia White born in 1864 and William born in 1873. Although no concrete evidence exists, long standing family tradition holds that Cornelia was fathered by her mother's master.

Whatever the circumstances, it did not appear to matter to Jim Chase. Soon after they met, Jim took Christina and her children with him on his journey to New England. For reasons that may never be known, Jim and Christina finally settled on Wickford, RI as the place they chose to call home. The first thing they did upon their arrival in the village was to marry. On January 7, 1875 Jim and Christina were married in Wickford. Their new life together had begun.

At the time of his marriage to Christina and at the birth of his daughter in 1876, Jim chase listed his occupation as "laborer". Again in 1880 when Chris-

Christina (White) Chase and her children, William and Cornelia White

tina gave birth to another child who died shortly after delivery, Jim called himself a laborer. But by the time of the 1885 Rhode Island Census, Jim and Christina's life had begun to change. They had just purchased their own home, and Jim was now listing his occupation as "teamster" (For the uninitiated, a teamster during the 1800s was not a unionized truck driver, but a man who was in charge of a "team" of draft animals {i.e. horses, oxen, or mules} and handled them as they hauled their loads.). Their home was the Thomas House (no relation) on Bay Street in Wickford; even then, the oldest home in the village. I can only imagine how proud they must have felt.

By now, the Chase family had lived in Wickford for ten years and were well liked and respected members of the community. Mary, their daughter, attended school at the Wickford Academy, where she was the only African-American student in her grade. A class photo from this timeframe is below. Jim was a member of the Charles Baker chapter of the GAR, a group very similar to today's VFW but open exclusively to Civil War veterans, which met at the Grand Army of the Republic Hall in Wickford. Although not solely without precedent, the fact that Jim, a black man in a world that was still very white, was a respected and accepted member of the local GAR chapter speaks volumes about his place in the community.

Below: Members of the Charles C. Baker Post of the Grand Army of the Republic (G.A.R.) of Wickford, R.I.

Right: Close-up view of James Chase

Mary Chase (third from right in second row) is shown in front of the Wickford Academy in a class photo circa 1885.

Some time shortly after the enumeration of the 1885 Rhode Island State Census, Jim came up with an idea which not only allowed him to provide a good life for his family, but also made him a regional celebrity of sorts. Jim Chase became "Jim Chase the Yeast Man" as he began to grow and market baker's and brewer's yeast out of his Bay Street home. Jim eventually became known throughout the region as the man to see for yeast.

About the same time Jim was making his mark as "The Yeast Man," his daughter Mary, was getting married to Charles Thomas of East Greenwich. They lived in the spacious "Old Yellow" with Jim and Christina and, in 1895, had a daughter which they named Florence Elizabeth Thomas. Sadly, for reasons unknown to this writer, things did not work out between Mary and Charles and, very atypically for the time, they were divorced. Charles moved on and was no longer a part of Mary or Florence's lives.

Life went on for the extended Chase family after Charles left. Florence followed in the footsteps of her mother and went to school at the

Mary (Chase) Thomas and her daughter Florence circa 1899.

Mary (Chase) Thomas and her daughter Florence

Above: Florence Thomas's graduation photo. Right: Clarence VanHagen in his World War I uniform circa 1917.

Wickford Academy. Mary began a decades long career as a midwife and childcare provider. Jim just went on being the Yeast Man and Christina kept the whole household running. Florence eventually married a young "doughboy" named Clarence Van Hagen and waited out WWI while he served out his time in the trenches. Clarence survived the "Great War", but tragedy struck the Chase family none the less when Jim Chase, the slave turned respected veteran and highly regarded local businessman died at the age of seventy-five. He was buried with military honors in one of the graves that surround the big GAR monument at Elm Grove Cemetery. Christina lived for another nine years and then was reunited with her husband at the age of eighty-two. She too, is buried in Elm Grove.

Again, the Chase family persevered. Mary, her sister Cornelia – known to all as Neelie, and her daughter and son-in-law filled "Old Yellow" with the sounds of a happy family. Ownership of the big house had been handed down to Mary upon the death of her parents. In 1931, the family's joy was doubled when Clarence and Florence were able to purchase the 1785 gambrel-roofed Peck-Freeborn House on Main Street just in front of Mary's "Old Yellow." By then, the family had already owned the circa 1735 house for forty-six years.

Their life went on in the usual way until 1954 when ninety-year-old Neelie, the daughter of a slave and a slave owner joined her parents and brother on their final journey to God. In 1965, Mary and Florence lost another family member when Clarence, too, went on to the next world. He, like his father-in-law, was seventy-five. Ninety-year-old Mary, and her seventy-year-old daughter were all that was left. They realized that two houses made no sense, and in 1966, after eighty-one years of continuous ownership they reluctantly sold "Old Yellow." Mary moved in with her daughter in the smaller Peck-Freeborn House.

At this time in Mary's life, I was lucky enough to cross paths with her. Not only did she appear like clockwork each Sunday at St. Paul's Episcopal Church where I also attended, I also saw either her or Florence each Saturday when I collected for the newspapers I delivered each evening. In spite of the fact that their paper occasionally ended up in the shrubs in front of the little house, they were as gracious with their errant paperboy as they were with everything else in their lives.

Mary and Florence continued to live on their own for nearly ten more years. Just prior to Mary's 100th birthday they were set up in a room together in the nearby Lafayette Nursing Home. In 1976, ninety-one years after they bought their first home in the village, the little house on the corner of Main and Bay Streets was sold to help pay for their care. The Chase/Thomas era in Wickford was over.

Sadly, shortly after Mary and Florence were set up as roommates at the nursing home, Mary suffered a tragic loss. Her daughter, and companion for some eighty years, took a quick turn for the worse and died. Mary was now alone after outliving all of her relations. Florence's obituary poignantly said it all with its last sentence, "Her 100 year old mother is her only survivor."

A few years later, Mary not only outlived all her family, but her money as well, and she was forced to move out of the town she loved so much. Those who knew her, feared that this above all other things would finally break her heart. She lived out her last years at the Bannister House in Providence. When she finally left this world on that early spring day in 1985, she was Rhode Island's oldest citizen and a symbol of local African-American pride. This last distinction, according to all that knew her, made her somewhat uncomfortable. You see, in her eyes she was just a Wickford girl, nothing more than that.

Mary's obituary ends with a sentence very similar to that of her daughter's. "There are no immediate survivors." But I must differ. She was survived by a village that loved her and counted her as one of their own for more than 100 years. She was survived by a statewide community of Black Americans who saw her life as an example of what can be accomplished through perseverance. She was survived by a retired banker, who was a close friend and neighbor, and took care of her affairs for years; he still speaks wistfully of the times he shared with her. And she was survived by a young paperboy who grew up marveling at the very notion of what it must be like to live so long and experience so much.

As I did my research for this story I decided to see if Mary was one of America's oldest citizens, as well as Rhode Island's, at the time of her death. I learned two things from this exercise. First, although Mary was not America's oldest citizen when she passed on, you could count those older than her at that time and not run out of fingers. Second, and most profoundly, I was struck by the undeniable fact that the large majority of the country's oldest citizens at this juncture in history were, like Mary, the children of slaves. This includes the two oldest, 115-year-old Willie Duberry of South Carolina and 114-year-old Susie Brunson of North Carolina. After much thought I've decided that the reason for this must be that no one could possibly appreciate freedom as much as the child of a slave. And they clung stubbornly to it, refusing to let go of what their parents had worked so hard for. Rest in Peace, Mary, Rest in Peace.

Mary (Chase) Thomas celebrating her 100th birthday.
Photo by David Perrotta, courtesy The Standard Times.

NORTH KINGSTOWN'S TIES TO "TWELVE YEARS A SLAVE"

All of North Kingstown should have stood up and taken notice as the groundbreaking and moving film "Twelve Years a Slave" was receiving its accolades at the 2014 Oscar Ceremony. For you see, the very roots of this stunning historical drama about a free black man in the mid-1800s, Solomon Northup, who was kidnapped and sold into slavery in Antebellum Louisiana, are firmly set in the soil of our fair town.

Solomon Northup's father Mintus Northup, as it turns out was born a slave, right here in North Kingstown, on the Northup homestead farm located on the southern side of the Annaquatucket River. The circa 1690 farmhouse in which Mintus' owners, first Col. Immanuel Northup and then his son Capt. Henry Northup resided, is still extant on Featherbed Lane. Immanuel Northup, a prominent farmer, landowner, and officer in the Rhode Island colonial militia, was born in 1700 and, as most large scale farmers did back in that time frame, utilized slave labor to operate his agricultural enterprise, spread across hundreds of acres here in what was then known as Kingstowne. On the census taken in 1774, Immanuel Northup is listed as owning seven slaves; among those must have been Mintus' parents and/or grandparents. Immanuel lived a long and prosperous life, outliving three different wives; one of those wives, Sarah (Gould), bore Immanuel a son Henry. Henry grew up in the big Northup homestead house and, upon reaching the age of majority, chose a life at sea; eventually achieving a captain's rating. He took a local gal, Mary Gardner as his wife and often sailed out of nearby Newport.

Throughout the Revolution, all of these members of this branch of the Northup family were quiet Loyalists; they kept their Tory leanings to themselves and after the War's end chose to stay on here in America. In 1790, as Immanuel's life wound down to its end, it appears he transferred ownership of most of his slaves to Henry as he is then listed owning five and Immanuel only two. A few months after this 1790 census, Colonel Immanuel Northup breathed his last breath and subsequently in his will required that his last two slaves to be given their freedom. Henry, who was the executor of his father's estate and who inherited substantial property including a portion of the Northup Homestead farm as well as Fox Island just off the coast of North Kingstown, sold off most of his assets and moved with his wife and family, along with his only retained slave Mintus to Hoosick Falls, New York where he purchased a farm of several hundred acres. Mintus worked the farm along with his master until he too, was freed upon Henry's sudden death in 1798. Mintus, now a free black, eventually married another free black Susannah and they had a son who they named Solomon, the eventual hero and author of the 1853 narrative memoir *Twelve Years a Slave* upon which this movie is based. Mintus, as a free man, took a position at the farm of his former master's nephew Clarke Northup in nearby Granville, NY and eventually settled in Hudson Falls where he lived out the remainder of his days, passing on in 1829.

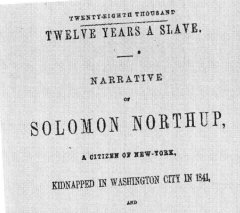

TWENTY-EIGHTH THOUSAND

TWELVE YEARS A SLAVE.

NARRATIVE

OF

SOLOMON NORTHUP,

A CITIZEN OF NEW-YORK,

KIDNAPPED IN WASHINGTON CITY IN 1841,

AND

RESCUED IN 1853,

FROM A COTTON PLANTATION NEAR THE
IN LOUISIANA.

NEW YORK:
MILLER, ORTON & MULLI(
26 PARK ROW, OPPOSITE ASTOR HOUSE.
AUBURN:
107 GENESEE STREET,
1855.

Title page and frontispiece from the book Twelve Years A Slave: Narrative of Solomon Northup, A Citizen on New-York, Kidnapped in Washington City in 1841, and Rescued in 1853, From a Cotton Plantation Near the Red River in Louisiana.

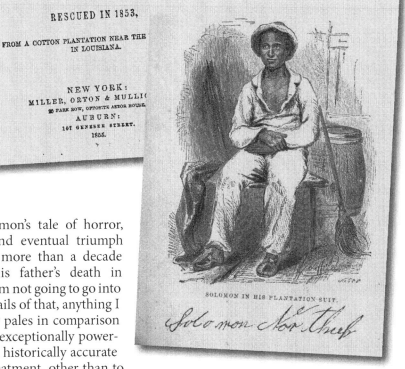

SOLOMON IN HIS PLANTATION SUIT.

Solomon's tale of horror, woe, and eventual triumph begins more than a decade after his father's death in 1841. I'm not going to go into the details of that, anything I can say pales in comparison to this exceptionally powerful and historically accurate film treatment, other than to point out that the person who eventually travels to Louisiana to confirm the truth of his status as a free man of color is Clarke's son, Henry B. Northup; a man named in honor of Mintus' former master.

Back on the banks of the Annaquatucket River at the time of Henry's move to upstate New York, the Northup Homestead farm was left in the hands of Henry's younger half-brother, Carr Northup, who in turn passed it down to his son Nicholas Carr Northup. In the late 1830s, just prior to Solomon losing the freedom that was his birthright down in the deep south, the heirs of Nicholas Carr Northup were selling the last portions of the once expansive

The Northup family plot at Elm Grove Cemetery.

Northup farm, including the ancient homestead house, to the Sanford family, who had plans to open a small textile mill there; powered by the very river that Northups settled upon. Later, as a part of the construction of that mill and the associated housing, including the fine Esbon Sanford millowner's home just across the lane from the Northup place, the Sanfords had the entire Northup family graveyard containing the remains of both masters and slaves, black Northups and white Northups, moved over to a newly purchased plot in Elmgrove Cemetery. I visit these folks from time to time over there in the quiet solitude of Elmgrove and contemplate their graves, the white Northups with their fine slate stones carved with care and precision in Newport, and the slaves of these folks, the very kin of Solomon Northup, marked only by simple fieldstones, and think about the very different lives they led.

Christiana Carteaux Bannister, by Edward Mitchell Bannister, courtesy Newport Art Museum.

CHRISTIANA BANNISTER

1819 was a memorable year for a hard working African-American/Narragansett Indian couple named John and Mary Babcock. They lived in the south west corner of North Kingstown, out past Slocumville, even out past Shermantown, in an area that was always known as "Dark Corners." Dark Corners nestled up against Stony Fort, and although Stony Fort was officially part of South Kingstown, everyone knew it to be Narragansett tribal land. It was the land of John and Mary's ancestor's and, although dark and foreboding to some, it probably felt like home to the Babcock's and their kin. 1819 was the year that Mary gave John a daughter. They named her Christiana. Little did they know then, but their daughter would one day leave her mark on the world in a most extraordinary way.

Nothing is known of Christiana's early life. What education she received she probably got at home, as the Dark Corners District Schoolhouse would not open until she was too old to take advantage of it. Somehow though, she learned what she needed to in order to succeed in life, because she next shows up in the historic records around 1850 as Madame Carteaux, the owner of a chain of upscale hair salons in Boston and Providence. These salons featured a line of cosmetics and skin and hair care products that she had invented. Perhaps they were the ancient secrets of the Narragansett Indian women, or maybe she came up with them all on her own; whatever the case they were wildly popular and had made her a prominent and successful black businesswoman in the time when such a thing was unusual. Even more unusual still was the fact that the majority of her clientele were the wealthy and prominent white women of the two cities. She was so successful in fact, that the abolitionist newspaper "The Liberator" profiled her in an issue from January of 1854. She had dropped her family name by then and went by the much more exotic sounding name of Christiana Carteaux. She may have let go of her Babcock roots, but she never lost touch with whom she was and where she came from. You see, besides being a successful businesswoman, Christiana was an activist. She worked fervently for a number of causes, chiefly, as you would expect, freedom for her people— the abolition of slavery.

Around the end of the 1840s, another talented and inspired young African-American was making his way from New Brunswick, Canada, to Boston. Edward Bannister, along with his brother William, had decided to head to America to pursue his life-long dream of becoming an artist. He had a natural talent as a barber, and eventually ended up working in one of Madame Carteaux's hair salons in order to put food on his table and to finance his quest to become a painter. Edward, too, was an activist, and he eventually became acquainted with his somewhat famous (not to mention attractive) boss. They fell in love and were married on June 10, 1857. They continued to work for causes they both cared about as a couple and championed the cause of equal pay for black soldiers who fought in the Civil War and held fundraisers to assist the widows and orphans of slain African-American soldiers. They were prominent and well-respected members of the Boston African-American community. They made a difference.

With his marriage to Christiana in 1857, Edward was finally financially sound enough to devote his entire attention to his passion for painting. Christiana's faith in him began to pay off soon after, as he began to get commissions and receive accolades for his talent. In later years, when speaking of this time and his wife's contributions to his success, he said, "I would have made out very poorly had it not been for her and my greatest successes have come through her."

By 1869, the atmosphere in Boston had changed to such a degree that the Bannisters decided to relocate to Christiana's home state to the south. The city reputation as a center for abolitionist activity and its relative benign acceptance of African-Americans had caused an influx of migration of former slaves. The resultant backlash from white residents who feared a loss of jobs and majority status forever changed the way the black man was viewed in the city. In October of that year they took up residence in Providence and would spend the rest of their lives there.

Edward Mitchell Bannister from The Colored American, May 25, 1901.

The move did little to change the lifestyle that the Bannister's were accustomed to. Christiana's hair salon empire was equally successful in Providence and they quickly became a part of not only the city's black community, but the growing art community as well. Edward and Christiana were instrumental in the founding of the Providence Art Club, as well as the now prestigious Rhode Island School of Design. But even with all that Edward was still only renowned as a regional artist. His big break came in 1876 at the Philadelphia Centennial Exposition, when his painting "Under The Oaks", which he entered in to the competition without notifying anyone that he was indeed a black man, took first prize. With this he became an artist of national renown.

All the while this was going on Madame Carteaux continued to run her hair and cosmetic business as well as pursue noble causes. In Providence she took up the cause of the fate of the city's elder black community and helped found the institution which is now named for her "Bannister House," a nursing home. She and Edward endowed the facility with a number of his paintings, including his portrait of her. They are presently on long term loan to the Newport Art Museum.

Edward's medal at the Centennial Exposition brought him fame and continued success. He was now among the most successful of black artists and continued to win awards and accolades. In spite of it all, he could never escape the shadow of prejudice that tainted his many successes. It has been said that Bannister's career was motivated by a desire to disprove a comment in the New York Herald which had incensed him. It stated "The Negro seems to have an appreciation of art, while being manifestly unable to produce it." Edward Bannister's life, as well as his work, emphatically denounces this stereotypical comment, and then some. He died at a prayer meeting at the Elmwood Street Baptist Church on January 9, 1901, of a massive heart attack. His last words were, "Jesus, help me."

Christiana's life took a rapid downward spiral from that point on. As they were childless, there was no one to look after her and she died penniless and alone at the State Hospital for the Insane in December of 1902. She was eighty-three.

The life of Christiana and Edward Bannister is still one of the many mysteries. How did a backwoods girl like Christiana Babcock manage to transform herself into the sophisticated Madame Carteaux? What happened to the substantial fortune that they had amassed; how could someone so successful die penniless? Also amazing is the fact that the majority of Bannister's most important works have disappeared from the art scene, including "Under The Oaks" his masterpiece. Where are they now? One thing though is certain. A little girl born in the backwoods of North Kingstown had grown up to change her world. And Bannister House, along with RISD itself, stands to this day as a testament to a life well lived.

The Roome Family

SLAVES TO SOLDIERS

Lately I've been taking a long hard look at the long ago lives of the folks that made up the Roome family. The history of the Roome family goes back to a time before there was a state of Rhode Island, back to colonial days. The first folks who called themselves Roomes came here, like most folks of the time, from across the Atlantic. The difference was though, that these immigrants came against their will, and until the moment the gavel fell at the auction in Newport or Bristol they weren't Roomes, as a matter of fact they probably weren't even related at all. The real names of this group of folks who were loaded into the back of a wagon belonging to London-born Newport businessman George Rome (pronounced Room) are lost to us forever. But from that momentous day onward, like it or not, they were a family. A family made up of the slaves of George Rome.

You know, it's hard to track the lives of folks who were once thought to be of such insignificance. These slaves were of value to Rome for sure; they were an investment counted on to bring in a return of sorts, not unlike a draft horse or a team of oxen. But lets face it, one does not record the daily triumphs and tribulations of a draft horse, no one marks the births, deaths, and important occasions within the lives of a team of oxen, so, needless to say, there is little permanent record on these people. I'm not even sure I know the names of the entire family group, although I do feel real comfortable calling them a family even though, as I said, they probably weren't even related. These displaced souls could only count upon themselves for solace; there was no one else they could turn to in times of need. When they experienced the rare peaceful or happy moment whom else would they share it with. If that's not what family is all about well I don't know what is. So, for better or for worse, the slaves of George Rome, real people who until then had had their own identities and their own names, but who for now and forever more would be known as Caesar, Cato, Pero, Juba, and Elizabeth got to know each other as they traveled to their new home across the Narragansett Bay; the summer estate of their master, at a place we now call Rome Point.

As I mentioned, at the present time, I know little of their lives as slaves. What I can tell you is that they tended to Rome's summer estate here in Kingstown under the direction of a overseer who also lived on the enormous piece of property that Rome had purchased at the bankruptcy of fellow Newporter Henry Collins. And when the newly formed government of the State of Rhode Island seized Rome's assets after convicting him of treason during the early days of the Revolution, his slaves were part of the property eventually purchased by

Ezekial Gardiner around 1778. I find it ironic to note that the proceeds of that sale, including the price paid for these slaves, went to help fund the war effort, the war effort to end British tyranny. And finally I can tell you that eventually these hard working folks too, got their freedom, when they were manumitted as required by Rhode Island law at the beginning of the 19th century. Caesar, Cato, Pero, Juba, and Elizabeth were finally free.

At this point in history, these folks start showing up in the historic record as real people. State and Federal censuses, beginning with 1800 call them free Negroes or free blacks. Town records record their living and dying, their births and marriages, and even the rare instances of property ownership. Old Pero as he was known, becomes a local character of sorts and is noted in numerous 19th century narratives. Cato Roome is involved tragically, in one of South County's most notorious crimes of the 19th century. They marry within the local African American/Native American community and have children and grandchildren. Most of their descendants live very ordinary lives, but some have their moments of greatness and become witnesses of and participants in the history of our country. And now that you know a bit about the Roome family background, we are going to zero in on the lives of two of the descendants of these former slaves, brothers James and John Roome.

The year was 1863 and James and John Roome, descended of Pero, had no doubt, just heard the exciting news about the all-colored regiment being formed up in Providence, to fight in the War against the south. It would be called the 14th RI Colored Heavy Artillery and was to be run by white officers under the command of Lieutenant Colonel Nelson Viall. These were exciting times for African Americans in the north, the tide had not yet turned in the war and all over the free north, black regiments were being formed up and people of color were to be allowed to take part in the War to end slavery. Their older cousin George, who had moved to Worcester, Massachusetts, had recently signed up in the 54th Massachusetts and was already training as James and John were making their mark on the enlistment papers in Providence.

Well, this may have been the north, and although there were no slaves here, things still weren't equal between the races and the first problem run into by Lt. Col. Viall was where was he to train his regiment of just over 2000 raw recruits. Many of the Regular Army, which trained in the capital city of Providence would not stand for the idea of training side by side with black men and so Viall needed to find another site. After conferring with the powers that be, he chose Dutch Island, just off the shores of North Kingstown, and ironically for the Roome brothers, within a stones throw of Rome Point for his training camp. It was to there that John and James headed in August of 1863. The moment was all the sadder for the recently married James as his wife Abby was seven months pregnant when he took the ferry over to Dutch Island that day.

After training, the 14th RI was assigned to the defense of New Orleans and the gulf of the great Mississippi River, just captured a year previous by the north under the command of David Farragut and David Porter as a part of a battle plan called "Anaconda." The idea was to squeeze the south by not only not allowing supplies up the Mississippi to the Confederacy, but also to constrict them financially by blocking the shipments of their only cash crop, cotton. The thinking was that if the south could not get its cotton to market their war machine would soon grind to a halt.

James and John's units were assigned to Fort Jackson, one of the two Forts stationed on either side of the Mississippi out at the very end of the delta. John, on a gun crew, was responsible for manning those heavy cannons and firing upon any Confederate flag or suspicious vessel attempting to run the blockade. James, had been assigned to the Quartermaster's Department, run by a white officer from his hometown, named John B. Peirce, a man who would one day be the Town Clerk of North Kingstown. Small towns being what they were (and still are) it in not unreasonable to suspect that Lt. John Peirce was already acquainted with his new assistant Private James Roome.

Lt. John B. Peirce

One of the greatest risks of being assigned to the twin forts, Jackson and Plaquemine, out in the swampy delta land at the end of the Mississippi was not death by bullet, but death by disease. The swampy mosquito infested quagmire that was the delta claimed more Union troops than the guns of the Confederacy, and sadly, James Roome was among them. In August of 1864, just a year after enlisting and ten months after the birth of a son he would never see, James Roome died of malarious fever and was buried in an unmarked grave in the Fort Jackson Cemetery. The epidemic claimed many Union lives including a white officer whose body was transported back to RI for burial. James was 26. Brother John continued on alone, serving also within the city of New Orleans proper during its occupation, until the unit was mustered out in October of 1865.

Both John Peirce and John Roome returned to Rhode Island and lived out their lives here. They both, undoubtably, told War stories to their families. I only hope that John Roome's tales of adventure were some comfort to young Henry James Roome as he grew up knowing that his father, descended from slaves, had given his life for the greater cause to free other slaves.

THE DEATH OF CATO ROOME

The death of Cato Roome was considered at the time to be one of the most notorious crimes in Rhode Island history and it was talked about around the village of Allenton, where Cato lived, for decades after. This version of the events of winter of 1837-38 was remembered by mill-owner William Pierce and recorded for posterity in Cole's History of Washington and Kent Counties which was compiled largely in 1888-9.

Pierce sets the tale by describing the two protagonists Cato Roome, an old feeble man of color who was well-liked and highly respected in the village of Allenton; he had recently undergone a surgery by Old Doc Shaw and was weakened by the ordeal, and James Browning, a stout robust black man of more than 250 pounds who ran a small successful farm. Cato Roome lived with his wife Dorcas, in a small home on the corner of what is now Tower Hill and West Allenton Roads and Browning's farm, which he shared with his wife and three sons was located about a half mile up what is now Pendar Road. Pierce tells the tale thusly, "The circumstances of the murder are as follows. Mr. Browning had been to Providence with a horse team carrying a load of poultry and farm produce and returning with winter stores. On his return he stopped at the house of Mr. Roome, late at night, complaining of feeling very bad and asked the old man to drive his team home for him and unload it. Cato declined saying he was not feeling well himself on account of his recent surgery. Browning then left and went on by himself. Some two or three hours later the old man Cato and his wife were awakened by the wife of Browning asking him to come with her to her house as her husband was acting very strangely, and had driven her out-of-doors, threatening to kill her. Cato went reluctantly, and arriving at the house was met in the entryway by Browning, who pounded him to death against the sides of the door threshold. Not being satisfied with this, Browning pounded Roome's head to jelly with a stone that had been used to hold the door open. The wife immediately alarmed the neighbors, who flocked to the scene of the tragedy (Pierce was among this group) and by sunrise some 50 people or so were on Browning's Farm. Soon after the murder, Browning, with his gun and his dog, had fled into the woods. Within an hour or so, Browning returned and threatened to start shooting. People sought shelter in and around the house and other buildings. His dog got to fighting with another dog eventually. This distracted Browning enough to allow the people there to rush him and overpower him. They carried him into the house and lashed him to the bedstead, it took as many men as could possibly stand around the bed to hold him down while he was being tied up. Once lashed to the bedstead, his only weapon was to spit which he did to anyone who entered the room. His mental health continued to deteriorate and he was finally carried off by the authorities to the jail in Kingston, where he died one month later, by then a complete raving maniac. He left behind a widow and three sons Samuel, Jonathan, and Daniel Browning. Daniel, too, went insane and killed his mother in March of 1846. He spent the remainder of his life at the State Farm in Cranston."

As is the case with most of the Roomes, no one knows now where Cato Roome is buried. No mention is made of how Dorcas Roome and her two grown sons, William and Ebenezer, dealt with this swirling maelstrom of tragedy, death, and insanity that had overcome their family and taken Cato. The tale does paint for us a picture of what life must have been like during a time when the only "law" around was a State Sheriff some ten miles away. Ironically, I also must note that the widow Dorcas Roome left this life in the same year and month that Daniel Browning murdered his widowed mother. In this manner too, the two families are forever tied together by tragedy.

THE STORY OF PERO ROOME

After obtaining his freedom along with the rest of his family towards the end of the 18th century, Pero apparently went where ever he could find work; drifting between North Kingstown and East Greenwich according to census records. It appears that along the way Pero must have married, as he is recorded to have had a son John, a deaf mute who eventually worked as a domestic in the Abby Updyke Hotel in East Greenwich, and a daughter Elizabeth, who married a cook from Philadelphia named John Williams in 1851. It is not completely clear from the twice-burned records gathering dust in our town hall, what Pero's wife's name was, but it appears to have been Sarah. At that time, they, along with most of the African-Americans residing in Wickford, lived in a small group of homes off of Fowler Street near Bush Hill Pond.

It was here that Pero's existence was first chronicled by Mrs. F. Burge Griswold in her memoirs entitled *Old Wickford – The Venice of America* written towards the end of her life and published in 1900. She described him as "short, square, grizzly-haired, and thoroughly African in features" and noted that he worked for her grandfather, "Old Doc" Shaw as a stable hand and general groundskeeper. She describes his wife as a large dowager-looking woman chronically ill from the effects of a tapeworm infestation and also mentions with fascination, their deaf and dumb son. It is apparent by the general tone of this section of her book that African-Americans at that time, were still thought of as being quite a bit inferior to the average Wickfordite of the 1830s.

Somewhere along the way between the 1830s and the late 1850s Pero's wife Sarah passed away and left him alone. Elizabeth, his daughter who had had a number of children with Henry Fairweather, a member of another local slave family, but never married until she joined up with John Williams, also moved on, as did Pero's deaf mute son John. Pero, had outlived all the other original Roome slaves and was now residing in a squatter's shack along the edge of the Ten Rod Road on land owned by Robert Rodman. No one, including Rodman, seemed to mind though. The area, a piece of land described as "less than desirable", eventually became known as "The Vale of Pero" and it was here that the old "grizzly-haired" gentleman lived his last days. His life was again chronicled, this time by Lafayette historian George Gardiner who described him as that "old Negro slave who was a relic of the Colonial days." As with most of the members of the Roome family, his death was not recorded and his final resting place is unknown. What is known however, is that two of Pero's grandsons grew up to fight in the ultimate war against slavery, the Civil War and in some way perhaps, avenged the injustices that Old Pero suffered. And the little undesirable plot of land along the Ten Rod Road, now largely filled in for an entrance road to an industrial facility, will always be known to some of us as the "Vale of Pero".

THE STORY OF GEORGE ROOME

George Roome was born in 1835, one of three children of Nathaniel Roome and his wife Deborah. I have not yet been able to, with 100% certainty, connect Nathaniel to the original known group of George Rome slaves, but all evidence points to Juba Roome as being the most probable father of Nathaniel. The Nathaniel Roome family next shows up in the historic record in the census of 1850. Nathaniel lists his occupation as a laborer and his three children's names are clearly indicated as George, Hannah, and Ellen. A decade later, in the 1860 Federal census, George Roome, now 24, is found residing on Millbrook St. in Worcester, Massachusetts, with his Rhode Island born wife Betsey and their one-year-old daughter Luella, who had been born in Massachusetts. One fact, which can be clearly gleaned from this 1860 document, is unusual. Betsey is listed in this and every census henceforth in her long life, as a white woman and her child Luella, and all of George and Betsey's subsequent children, is listed as a mulatto. Now, a little aside about the word "mulatto." I'm sure most of you have come across it before and probably are aware that it indicates a person born of one white and one black parent, and was used extensively throughout the 18th and 19th century, showing up in that timeframe as an official race designation on all government documents, including the census. What you may not be aware of is the root derivation of this word. It began its life as derogatory slang word derived from the word mule; which as we all know is a sterile stubborn and somewhat slow-witted animal born of a horse and a donkey. Like many words that we now use without realizing their origin (the word denigrate also fits into this category), the passage of time has removed some of its painful sting, but believe me in the second half of the 19th century that label was not viewed so benignly. Getting back to George and Betsey, I have no idea whether the realities of being involved in a mixed marriage in the late 1850s had anything to do with their move from rural North Kingstown to the more anonymous metropolis of Worcester, Massachusetts, or if it was strictly an economic decision based on better employment opportunities. Whatever the case, George and Betsey must have had a "difficult row to hoe" no matter where they resided.

George Rome (he either purposely or through a US Army clerical error had dropped one "o" from his name at this time) next shows up in the historic record when he enlists, in May of 1863, in the 54th Regiment of the Massachusetts Volunteer Colored Infantry. His enlistment was probably motivated at that time by a combination of duty to his country, his people, and the entice-ments, as shown in the accompanying recruiting poster, of a $100 signing bo-nus, a regular paycheck of $13/month, and the promise (often never realized) of state aid for his family while he was gone. By the end of the month his unit was bound for battle, heading out of Boston Harbor on the steamer *DeMolay* off to Hilton Head, South Carolina.

Now, I won't go into a long description of the extraordinary accomplish-ments of the 54th Massachusetts. It's enough to say that it was often remarked, "that no unit, colored or white, fought more heroically than the men of the 54th." No one could tell their tale more powerfully than the Hollywood movie production "Glory" did, so if you're curious, rent this award-winning movie and see for yourself what these men accomplished. All that mattered to George, Betsey, and his children, is that he, unlike many of his comrades in arms, man-aged to survive the war, and returned in 1865 to their Millbrook Street home in Worcester.

According to census data taken after the war, George and Betsey's family grew to include 6 children. Beyond their first child Luella, I have identified a son Albert and two daughters Alice and Emma. After being a hero in the

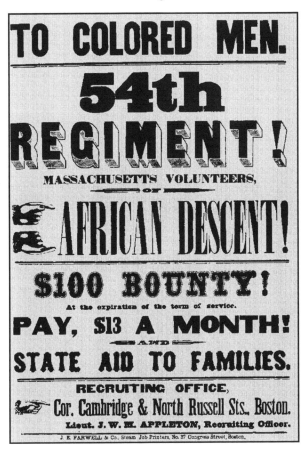

This poster, listing a number of enticements to encourage enlistment, was plastered on walls and lightposts all over New England.

Civil War, George returned to his normal life, always listing his occupation as a day laborer. Two of his daughters seemed to eventually marry and leave home, as Luella's last name became Potter, and Alice became a Clark. George Rome must have left this world between 1900 and 1910, as he does not show up in the records after the 1900 census. I don't know if a gravestone marks his final resting place or not. It could be that, beyond the monument to the 54th Massachusetts in Boston, the only concrete testimony to his existence is the same fine straight and true stone walls that memorialize the lives of his slave ancestors on their master George Rome's farm here in town. Whatever the case, he left his mark on the world none the less. His death, combined with the coming of the Great Depression seemed to bring his children back to their mother's side, as by 1920, Luella Potter and her daughter Olive, Alice Clark and her husband John and son Paul and the children of another daughter whose name is yet unknown are found to be living on Millbrook Street with 77 year old Betsey and her son Albert. Beyond 1920, I do not know what happened to George Rome's extended family, but I intend to find out. I can't help but admire this couple, a slave's grandson married to a white woman in the turbulent era of the Civil War. There must have existed a powerful connection between them to face what they must have and triumph as they did. This tale is more than a black history story, it's a love story as well.

I'll close this by revealing the last interesting detail of this remarkable story. As I said earlier, Betsey seems to have raised the children of one of her other daughters, one whose name I have yet to identify. The two children's names though are clearly written on the census form; a grandson named Benjamin George Walker and a granddaughter named Alice R. Walker. Now if that last name sounds familiar, don't be surprised, as the novel "The Color Purple" was written by an Alice Walker as well. And although I have yet to be able to decipher whether there is any connection between these two Alices, I feel certain that if I could ask either of them they would assure me that whether they are truly related or not, they are most certainly connected; connected by the shared experience that binds every black child to another, whether they realize it or not.

By the end of the 1800s the old Roome farm was owned by the Greene family, who still used a number of black farmhands, some of whom lived on the farm, and others nearby. One of these men is most certainly George Weeden as he shows up in census data as living with the Greenes. Thomas Artist, who lived in the vicinity of this farm, maybe in this group photo as well.

Everyday People

REFLECTIONS ON NUMEROUS RICHARD THOMASES

You know, I have got to tell you, I am a huge fan of actor Richard Thomas. Since his breakthrough role as John-Boy Walton in 1971 through numerous Hallmark Hall of Fame movies and television appearances, I have admired his work. Just between you and me, I even sort of identify with that John-boy character of his. Yup, if there is a Richard Thomas movie on television on any given night, chances are I am watching it.

For the last few years though, I have been thinking about Richard Thomas in a whole new light. You see, whenever "The Homecoming" or some other wonderful Hallmark Hall of Fame/Richard Thomas cinematic treasure captures my imagination in the confines of my warm comfortable living room, my mind can't help but wander off to Wickford in the mid-1800s. The scene in my mind's eye plays out like this; it's June in 1850, and an elderly dapper Wickford merchant is strolling with his wife down Main Street on a beautiful summer evening. They are both well dressed and impeccably groomed, befitting their status in this small prosperous village. Just before they reach the front door of their fine Main Street home they encounter a young black couple coming up Main Street from the Pleasant Street intersection. This couple is youthful and enterprising, but poor. It is obvious that they are to have a child soon and they both carry the aroma of the sea with them as they encounter the older pair. Their eyes meet as they walk and anyone can see that they all know one another at some level. Additionally, the demeanor of the two men indicates that there is some kind of larger unspoken connection between them. As they pass, the old merchant greets the young man and his pregnant wife with a sincerely spoken "Good evening Richard." The rugged plain spoken black man replies, "Good Evening to you Mr. Thomas." The two wives as well, exchange pleasantries, and then these couples head off on their way to their destinations.

The scene I just mapped out for you is a Main Street encounter between Wickford's two Richard Thomases. The elderly gent was well-known shopkeeper Richard Thomas whose wife's name was Polly. They lived and kept a dry goods store in what is now 60 Main Street; a house given to them by Richard's father Samuel Thomas. The young black couple was Richard Thomas the fish peddler and his wife was named Rachel. They lived at what is now 101 Pleasant Street. The house that exists there today consists of a heavily modified version of their small cottage, originally constructed around 1841 for this African-American couple, most probably the children of slaves. Richard Thomas earned his living as a local fish peddler and his wife Rachel, likely related to free black mariner Domini Smith who lived nearby on Fowler Street, worked as a domestic. Richard was most certainly the brother of Nancy Thomas who lived nearby in the still extant Thomas/Weeden/Morgan House. Although none of Richard and Rachel Thomas' children survived childhood it does appear that they raised the orphaned daughter of another African-American neighbor Ellen Berry, as census data shows her living in their home. White Richard and Polly had numerous children of their own, all of whom went to the finest schools and universities and had careers and lives that were appropriately prominent. Rachel died in 1883 and Black Richard, as he was known to avoid the obvious confusions, died in 1890. Their home and property were purchased by the neighbor just to the south, master housewright James Bullock who modified it into the fine home we see today. White Richard Thomas's home, along with the family business, was left to his son Allen Mason Thomas, who became an even more prominent Wickford community pillar than his father was. Beyond sharing exactly the same name and living in the same town at the same time, I expect their lives couldn't have been more different. I often wonder if Black Richard was present at the well attended graveside service for White Richard in August of 1859 out at Elmgrove Cemetery. Decades later when he buried his wife Rachel under a simple gravestone in an obscure corner of that same cemetery, did he wander by and admire the imposing obelisk erected to commemorate the lives of White Richard and Polly? As his adopted daughter Ellen Berry lowered Black Richard into a grave that to this day is still unmarked, did she look over at White Richard's monument and sigh? I sure would like to ponder these things with John-Boy Walton at my side someday, he'd have an answer for us I bet.

TWO OF THE BLACK GARDINERS

Back in the late 18th and the first half of the 19th century, the largest group of all, in our fair town, was the Gardiner family. There were numerous Gardiners living in every village that made up North Kingstown in that timeframe, and this large inter-related family was an integral part of the community decade upon decade. The truth of this can be found today in the cemeteries of North Kingstown; from the tiniest little historic cemetery lost in the deep woods to the great burying grounds at Elm Grove and Quidnessett, literally hundreds of Gardiners still rest eternal here in the town they called their own. Gardiners today have cause to be proud of those that went before them; those folks had a hand in making North Kingstown their ranks contain important political figures, revered judges, and master builders that left their mark on the town. One branch of the Gardiner family though, has largely been forgotten; no grand memorial stones mark their gravesites, little has been written regarding their accomplishments—or the trials and tribulations of their days on this earth. These folks are the descendants of the original slaves that worked on the six farms that made up the vast dairy empire of Judge Ezekiel Gardiner and his sons; the judge was a member of the Narragansett Planter elite and his enormous agricultural enterprise churned out literally thousands of pounds of cheese each year and all this required the efforts of numerous slaves. These folks upon their manumission took the last name of their master. These are the roots of the black Gardiners and we will delve into the lives of two of them sailors both, Tom Gardiner and Nathaniel Onion Gardiner; by remembering them we will bring them back to life, if only for a moment.

Thomas Gardiner was born sometime around 1808, the son of 15-year old Dorcas Gardiner and a yet unknown father. Dorcas herself was born to Richard and Sarah (Onion) Gardiner and was the cousin of Thankful (Onion) Union a woman whose life we also profiled. I know little about Tom's early days, only that he chose a life as a seaman and that he was very successful at it. At the moment of this untimely death on the Wickford-based Grand Banks cod fishing schooner *Metamora*, a 63-foot vessel owned by Wickford businessmen Eliphalet Young, Pardon T. Hammond, and William Hammond, and captained by another Wickfordite George Hammond, old Tom has amassed quite a little nest egg. The 46-year old left a home in which he lived with Dorcas, in addition to monies in a number of banks with the 2014 inflation adjusted cash equivalent of $109,000. Old Tom Gardiner was buried at sea in the "Bay of Islands" off of Newfoundland. His mother Dorcas, who had passed away unbeknownst to him while he was off fishing for cod, was buried under a gravestone paid out of Tom's estate.

Nathaniel Onion Gardiner was born to Margaret Onion around the same time as Tom and was the brother of aforementioned Thankful. Nat's father, whose exact identity is unknown, was a Gardiner and upon reaching adulthood, Nat Onion changed his name to Nat Gardiner. He, too, chose a life at sea and like his cousin Tom, the sea took him when it wished. According to Warren, Rhode Island ship's agent Randolpheus Johnson, Nathaniel Gardiner died at sea onboard the 89-foot bark *Hector* off the coast of Zanzibar, an island nation on the eastern coast of Africa in July of 1851. He was buried there at sea by his Captain, Wheaton Cole. His family back in Wickford was not informed of his death for three full years until the *Hector* finally returned to Warren, its homeport.

NORTH KINGSTOWN RUNAWAYS

Most of my friends and relations seem to feel that I have a penchant for making some very obscure selections when it comes to reading materials. I can't quite understand this; why, during this long holiday weekend I passed the time pouring over the details of this very interesting two-volume work entitled *Runaways, Deserters, & Notorious Villains* written by noted Providence historian and photo archivist Maureen Taylor. These books are a compilation of all the advertisements placed in 18th century RI newspapers regarding runaway slaves, wives, and apprentices, as well as deserters form the Revolutionary War and a few escaped prisoners thrown in for good measure. From these advertisements, it is possible to glean all sorts of interesting tidbits of information regarding life in 18th century North Kingstown. With all this going for them, for the life of me I can't understand why they aren't on any bestsellers list.

So what did we learn from these advertisements? As far as runaway slaves go, as expected in a community with more than its fair share of slaves, there were quite a number—19 to be exact. There would be quite a few more were it not for the division of the town into North and South Kingstown during this period, as there were even more slaves in our sister community to the south. Lodowick Updike at Smith's Castle lost his slave Dimas, in April of 1763; he described him as a "subtle fellow with a forged pass" and is willing to pay $6 to get him back. At the other end of town, Phebe Browning lost four of her slaves, Rose and infant, Nancy and Jenny, in 1799 and will only pay ten cents reward for reach. She describes them in some detail and proclaims that Jenny is a "wench." Also in the southern end of town, Willett Carpenter lost two slaves in 1799, one named Cezar and the other with the very odd moniker of Hand-saw. He offers up a $5 reward for each. Down in Wickford, Immanuel Case advertised the loss of his slave Cuff who he describes as a "short thickset fellow with a long-built head." The most valuable slave advertised was Warren who belonged to John Barber and was trained as a merchant seaman. In 1780 a reward of $120 was offered the capture of this "fellow who is exceedingly black with a greasey look." Most likely Barber "rented" Warren out to ship owners and this loss of income caused him to offer up a large reward. Although slaves were not the only runaways listed in this intriguing book, their listings do offer us quite a bit of information about attitudes in that timeframe.

THE STORY OF THANKFUL UNION

Thankful Union, the minute I first saw that name I just knew there had to be a special story associated with it. Thankful Union is a departed soul who is buried in the "potter's field" section of Elm Grove Cemetery. As detailed in Althea McAleer's book on the cemetery, all that is known about her is that she was "a colored mute" who died in 1881 at the age of 95 years old. Thankful's name and circumstances have intrigued me; and I have felt compelled to find out what she, and her life, was all about. I must say though, that this was a difficult task. Few records were kept concerning the births, lives, and deaths of African-Americans in the 18th and 19th centuries; in this regard, they lived in a shadow world, leaving little concrete evidence of their very existence behind. This is truly frustrating for the historical researcher, but in a large sense it is a sad statement about America and the times. But Thankful and her extended family were different, and through, what I can only consider an act of divine providence, I have been able to piece together something of her life. I must add here, that as the facts are few, only the long dead players in this fascinating tale know for certain if I have got it 100% correct, but I do feel confident that I have gotten the gist of her story right.

To understand the journey which brought Thankful to her inevitable end in the pauper's section of our fair town's major burial ground, you have to go back two generations, and you must know that Thankful Union was not her given name; she was born with the same slave name as the man with whom we begin this tale, her grandfather Johnny Onion. John Onyun (he spelled it in this phonetic fashion) first shows up in the permanent record on a tattered and burned piece of paper in the vault in the North Kingstown Town Hall proclaiming his marriage to a woman of color from Jamestown known as Jemima. Let me pause here in our story to let you know that all reference to African-Americans in the permanent record from this timeframe are tagged with either the phrase "a man (woman) of color" or as a Negro man or woman. No other reference to John and Jemima Onion seem to have been recorded and the story now continues with their children and their children's families. It would appear that John and Jemima had at least three children. The record shows two sons named Cezar and Frazee, and a daughter named Freelove, and perhaps a daughter or daughter-in-law named Sarah. Cezar and Frazee, upon reaching adulthood, moved to Exeter and married, respectively, Jane and Eunica (surnames unrecorded). They lived long lives in Exeter and were active members of the Exeter Baptist Church. Cezar's wife, Jane, died in 1827 and he remarried a woman from the church named Nancy. Nancy was known as Nannie Onion and was probably a long-serving nanny to the family of James Sheldon, as she is mentioned in his will. But our story is about John and Jemima's daughter and granddaughters, so we will leave Frazee and Cezar for now, although not for good.

Freelove had five children that I know of, a son Nathaniel, and daughters Freelove, Margaret, Sarah, and Eunice. Our story now turns to two of those daughters, Margaret and Sarah. Margaret and Sarah Onion must have been remarkable women. They lived in a fairly affluent village, as Wickford was at the time, and probably held domestic positions in some of the prominent homes. The facts seem to support, as you will soon see, that Margaret worked for the Gardiner family, but there is no way of knowing for whom Sarah worked. It appears that they raised families as single mothers, the records clearly and undeniably show that Margaret's two sons were fathered by a man named Richard Gardiner and no mention of a husband can be found for Sarah, although considering the condition of North Kingstown's records there is a small chance that she was married. I tend to doubt this, though, as three separate references to Sarah and her three children, Nathaniel, Ishmael, and Thankful, can be found with no corresponding mention of a husband/father. The birth date that I have for Sarah's youngest, Thankful, I can only infer a year from her death information, 1786. Sadly, in August of 1803, Sarah Onion died, leaving her three children, all under the age of 21, parentless. The North Kingstown probate court appointed a guardian for them, one Benjamin Davis, but his job was only to see that they got placed in an appropriate home; and the records indicate that Margaret's family was where they ended up. Where Margaret housed this large family of one woman and five children prior to 1817 is unknown. But, in 1817, a remarkable turn of events changed the lives of Margaret and her, by then, mostly adult children forever. First, Richard Gardiner, the father of Margaret's two sons, died without a will, and secondly, Margaret Onion, an African-American domestic, living quietly in the world of 19th century Wickford, put up a bid of $21.00 on a piece of property being auctioned off from Gardiner's estate to settle his debts, and, against all odds, won the bid. Margaret Onion, a single black woman in a decidedly white man's world, was the lawful owner of a house on one-sixteenth of an acre on an unnamed side street in Wickford. One can only image the wonderment and celebration which must have reigned across the extended Onion family in both Wickford and Exeter on that day. Nearly two hundred years later I swear I could still feel pride as I read the real estate record in the dusty ledgers of the town hall.

Time marched on for the Onion family, but it did so in such a fashion as to not have left a single footprint in the permanent record, that is until the 1850s. By now, Margaret has apparently joined her sister, brothers, and parents in the next world and no record of the fate of her little home can be found. It was either demolished or most probably the real estate records detailing its fate were lost in the fire that damaged so many of North Kingstown's archived records. Nathaniel Onion Gardiner and his sister Thankful were now living in another home on Washington Street, purchased by Nathaniel through a real estate exchange that went unrecorded at that time or was lost in the same blaze that may have destroyed the records relating to their Aunt's home.

Nathaniel Gardiner was born Nathaniel Onion, the son of Sarah Onion and an unknown father in 1803. Sarah Onion died suddenly and Nathaniel and his sister Thankful became the wards of their Aunt Margaret Onion and her common law husband Richard Gardiner, who was descended from the slaves of Narragansett planter Ezekial Gardiner. When Nathaniel came of age, he took the last name of his adopted father and began a life as a merchant seaman under the name of Nathaniel Gardiner. Nat Gardiner died at sea onboard the 89 ft. barque *Hector* and was buried at sea in 1851. His family was not notified of his death until years later when the *Hector* returned to the Narragansett Bay. The house and Nathaniel's worldly possessions were left to his sister Thankful Onion who by that time was working as a domestic for Allen Mason Thomas. To allow the probate transfer to occur, A.M. Thomas, acting as the agent for the estate of Nat Gardiner, arranged for the official recording of the real estate transaction between the Case family, in the persons of John P. Case's grandchildren Elizabeth Brenton Shaw and John Peck Case Shaw, and Nathaniel Onion Gardiner. This transaction, in which the house was described as the "Sambo place", allowed legal ownership of the home to be transferred to Thankful Onion. Thankful lived in the home until 1870 when she sold the home to John P. and Mercy Lewis. Thankful, lived out most of the rest of her days in the home of Allen Mason Thomas; spending only her last year at the Town Farm where she died in 1881. At sometime she changed her last name from Onion to Union, more than likely in celebration of the Emancipation Proclamation. I have no idea when and why she became a mute, although no one could ever blame her if she just chose never to speak again, but that is, until now, the only thing we knew of her. That was her epitaph for more than 100 years—Thankful Union, a colored mute. The irony of her name and her last years continued to haunt me. I can think of only two things I can do to make it up to here; one, I have done by telling her story, and the other, well, somewhere out there under the thick grass which covers the potter's field at Elm Grove, sadly she was not even buried with all her family out in the graveyard on Cezar's land in Exeter,

This slip of paper was delivered to Nat Gardiner's next of kin three years after he sailed off from Wickford.

is a small marble stone erected by the town in 1881 to mark yet another of the graves of one of the folks who lived their lives out at the poor farm. It may take me awhile but I plan to find it this spring and stand it up to face the sun.

THOMAS WILLIAM ARTIST

Thomas William Artist was born in Virginia in December of 1844 to Henrietta Artist and an unnamed father. It is unknown at this time whether Thomas was born free or into slavery. He next turns up in Providence as 20 year old when he signs up for service in the 14th Rhode Island Heavy Artillery, an all black unit commanded by white officers that drew countless young black men from not only Rhode Island and Massachusetts, but also New York and Virginia to the state for the opportunity to fight in the Civil War. Artist's service period, from February to October of 1865, insures that he was sent to the Deep South and served in the defense of New Orleans and Plaquemine Parish in Louisiana. He was mustered out in New Orleans in October of 1865 and returned to Rhode Island where he spent the rest of his life. In 1876, Artist, who had been working regularly in North Kingstown, Jamestown, and on Block Island as a farm laborer, married Lucy Sheffield, daughter of John Sheffield of Block Island, and brought her back to the small farm he had purchased in Saunderstown village here in North Kingstown; half of which he had purchased from the Rose family in 1874 and the other half from the Carpenter family in 1875. Thomas was no longer a farm laborer, he was a farmer. Thomas and Lucy never had children and they spent the rest of their days working their small Saunderstown farm. Lucy died in June of 1908 and was buried in Elm Grove Cemetery. Thomas remarried in 1910 and he and his second wife Emeline, continued to work the farm and supplement their incomes by taking in boarders. In May of 1916, Thomas Artist died of heart failure, he was 71 years old. As detailed in his will, his entire estate was liquidated upon his death and all of his assets, including the farm itself, were converted to cash, and, with the exception of two $500 behests to relatives of his first wife, both of whom still lived on Block Island, donated to "the Colored Children's Shelter in Providence". The only other cash outlay noted in his will, except for the payment of his debts, was to provide for the creation of a fine headstone for he and Lucy; a stone that made note of his service in the Nation's Great War against slavery.

The estate of Thomas Artist, although nearly all of its worth was donated to charity, did provide for this fine gravestone which proudly attests to his service during the Civil War.

EDWARD LAFOREST GRANDERSON

Edward Laforest Granderson, who went by his middle name, was born in 1823 to Abraham and Mary (Hall) Granderson. Mary, his mother, was probably a descendant of the slaves of the Hall family, one of the regions earliest settlers, and Abraham was purported to have been born in Trinidad. After Abraham's death, Mary married a Robinson. They lived in a small house on the south side of Stony Lane near its intersection with the Boston Post Road on land that once been owned by the same Hall family that had owned Mary's ancestors. Laforest worked with his father in his youth as a farm laborer, but by the time of the 1850 census, the 27 year old was calling himself a fisherman.

Sometime during the 1850s he met and married Betsey Watson, who was originally from Newport, and they had three sons together Daniel Watson, George Lincoln, and Charles Edward. Betsey was most likely of mixed race ancestry as a diary entry from the late 1880s describes her as "whiter than some white folks…I couldn't have told her from a white person, a tanned hard working white person." By 1860, Laforest was calling himself a farmhand and during that decade entered into the long term employ of Avis Ann Spink, who, as a widow woman, was running her family farm in Wickford. Betsey, throughout their marriage, worked as either a washerwoman or a housekeeper. One of the benefits of working on the Spink farm was that Avis Ann provided a home for the Grandersons to live in; the small house, which was located on the farm property near the top of Bush Hill just north of Wickford village proper, was eventually deeded over to the Grandersons by Avis Ann Spink, sometime around 1870. Laforest Granderson, worked for the remainder of his days on the Spink farm and died in the small house there in January of 1885. The house and property was left in equal shares to his three sons with a caveat that Betsey could live out her life there. Youngest son Charles bought out his two brother's shares and lived there with his wife Mary and mother Betsey. After the death of both of them, he sold the house in 1916. Charles died half a decade later and all three are buried without gravestones in Elm Grove Cemetery. Eldest son Daniel moved to Providence, where he owned a home sometime prior to his father's death and lived there for the rest of his life. He evidently was married for a time as in the 1920 US Census he is listed as a 70 year old widower living with 59 year old widow Eliza Thomas. Daniel died sometime in the 1920s. Middle son George lived near the intersection of Oak Hill Road and Tower Hill Road and worked as a laborer and bricklayer for most of his life. He was married to Nellie (Robinson) and had a son, George Edward in July 1916 and a daughter Louse. George, who worked with his father, was a WWII veteran. George Lincoln Granderson died in February of 1942 and is buried in the Potters field section of Elm Grove Cemetery with no gravestone. George Edward Granderson, who was married to Essie (Phillips) owned a home on Post Road on a lot that now contains a fast food restaurant. His death in May of 1969 spelled the end of more than 120 years of Granderson's residing in North Kingstown. He is buried next to his father in Elm Grove Cemetery.

HENRY MCPHERSON

Henry McPherson was born a slave around 1808 in Washington DC to Celia McPherson and an unidentified father. The story behind his early years is, as of yet, unknown; he does, however, show up in Wickford in the 1830s working as one of the numerous black mariners sailing out of the village at that time. In 1844, he purchases a parcel of land in the backwoods on a cart trail that ran from the area around the head of West Main Street through the woods until it intersected with the Ten Rod Road at Lafayette. The southern section of that old cart trail is now known as Hendrick Avenue. The McPherson parcel was about an acre in size and local history books suggest that he was just one of a number of black property owners living out there at the time. Henry, leaving a life as a mariner in that same time frame and beginning a career as a laborer/farmhand, lived there with his wife Mary and the seven children they eventually had together Mary T., Isabella, Celia, Elizabeth, Charles, Eliza, and John B. Eldest daughter Mary T. married black mariner George Dailey of Thompsonville, Ct, in December of 1865 and left the area, Elizabeth married James Weeden in the late 1860s and moved to Providence. Eliza died of tuberculosis in 1865 at the age of 16. The fate of daughters Isabella and Celia are unknown. In 1870 son Charles wedded a girl named Mary and relocated to East Greenwich where he worked as a farmhand. They have at least two children, Alonzo born in March of 1871 and Mary J. born in 1879. John B. shows up in the census records as having moved in with his sister Elizabeth and her husband James Weeden in Providence in 1870 where the 15 year old also works as a farm laborer. By 1880, he is back in North Kingstown with a wife named Abby and two young daughters Elizabeth and Charity sharing a home with the family of William Reynolds, a 49 year old black man and his second wife Mary G., who was also in her second marriage; as also listed in the house are step-children Fred, Andrew, and Isabella Jourden, along with a two year old son William H. Reynolds. It may be that 49 year old William is Abby's father. Henry McPherson died on December 10th, 1877 from the same scourge that took his daughter Eliza, tuberculosis. His wife sold the plot of land and home that they owned together for more than thirty years and disappeared from the historic record. In a bit of irony that is unfathomably sad, by 1885, his grandson Alonzo McPherson began a life as a career criminal serving his first term of incarceration in the RI State Prison at the age of 15. He would be arrested and sentenced to the same jail four more times, all for armed assault and armed robbery. I cannot help but be glad that Henry did not live to see this turn of events; the grandson of a slave, who through extraordinary effort and determination lived a life as a mariner and homeowner, through his own actions returns to a life of almost total bondage. Alonzo McPherson died of chronic kidney disease in February of 1931.

URIAH RHODES WEEKS

Uriah Weeks was born in Warwick, RI, in 1821 to William and Sarah Weeks; across the years he appears to have changed the spelling of his surname as later in his life he and his family are often identified as "Wicks" or "Wickes". He shows up in the historic record in an 1855 state census in New York City, married to Sarah, who is listed as a native of Connecticut and working as a barber/hairdresser. In 1856, they have their first child, a son they name Willie. By 1858, they have relocated back to Rhode Island, where Uriah opens up a barber shop in Wickford. In 1859 Uriah and Sarah have their second child, a daughter they name Ida. Tragedy strikes the family in July of 1862 when their six year old son accidentally drowns. The sad tale is picked up by the national press and run literally all over the nation. This excerpt from a newspaper in New Bern, North Carolina is typical; Willie, son of Uriah Weeks, the barber of Wickford, left his home just before night on Tuesday, with his toy boat to sail it on the cove, and while engaged in his sport, slipped in and was drowned between the two bridges. His body was recovered on Wednesday morning; he was six years of age.

Uriah Weeks served the hairdressing needs of the black community in South County from 1858 until 1871 and was prominent and successful enough to warrant listing in the Providence business directory for many of those years. During this period Uriah and Sarah had three more children, all sons, Frank D., Arthur W., and Ernest G. In 1872, the Weeks family, now using the name Wicks, moved to Providence where Uriah opened up a new barber/hairdressing establishment. Two years later, Uriah contracted pneumonia which led to his sudden death on May 3rd, 1874. He was only 53 years old. The family shows up in the historic record in the 1880 census with Sarah living on Cushing Street in Providence and sharing her home with her adult daughter Ida Monro, Ida's two young daughter Louisa May and Nina, and her sons Frank, Arthur, and Ernest. Frank at 18 years of age was employed as a hotel bellboy, Arthur at 16 was an apprentice wheelwright, Ernest was in school, and Sarah and Ida worked together as laundresses and housekeepers. The very last record found concerning this family is a death record noting Ernest's death in 1895 from Typhoid Fever. He was 23.

NEWPORT PHILIPS

I have no idea exactly when during the mid-1700s that Newport Philips entered this world but I do know the "where" and the "what" of his very beginnings. What he was, from the instance of his birth, was a slave, and where he endured that servitude was on the enormous Philips farm centered around their manor house "Mowbra Castle." The Philips family was most assuredly among the landed gentry of the region; and although they are never mentioned as members of the Narragansett Planter elite, I've got to say that I'm not sure

The Mowbra Castle was the manor house for the Philips family during the period that Newport and Jack Philips were slaves here.

why not. Philips' landholdings in the 18th century were measured in the hundreds and hundreds of acres, the Mowbra Castle was arguably the largest and finest home on the West Bay, and finally and most importantly, their agriculturally focused business dealings were accomplished throughout the period with ample quantities of slave labor. Newport Philips was one of those slaves.

Early on in his existence, no written record exists of the milestones in his life. With the exception of perhaps the financial ledgers of their owners such things were not deemed worthy of notation – no one goes down to the Town Clerk and records the birth of an ox or the marriage of a good herd dog, why take that effort with a slave. But then in March of 1789, something quite remarkable occurred something worthy of recording in the permanent record of our fair town, something actually worthy of a celebration, the most momentous event, for certain, in Newport Philips' life happened; his owner it seemed had a change of heart. Newport Philips, once owned by Samuel Philips, was the property of Peter Philips. Peter Philips for reasons now unknown, transferred ownership of Newport to neighbor Beriah Waite and in that month both men went down to the Town Clerk and proceeded to do something life changing for Newport and slave brethren Jack Phillips – they legally set them free. The legal term for this is manumission; Beriah Waite filled out an order of manumission for Newport Philips and Peter Philips did the same for Jack. Additionally they both put up a $100.00 bond as a surety guaranteeing that Newport and Jack would do nothing as free men to break the laws of the State of Rhode Island. Both documents, recorded by Town Clerk George Thomas and witnessed by Benjamin Davis, mentioned "setting him free to his own use and liberty" done in "recognition and consideration of good servitude and labour." In other

The manumission record of Newport Philips

words Newport and Jack as of that day were not only free men but they were entitled to whatever they earned for themselves, they owed no man anything. Certainly a copy of these certificates was given to each man and they were sent on their way grasping the most important piece of paper ever.

Newport seems to have stayed in North Kingstown for a time, but by 1800 he is living as a free black man in Portsmouth Rhode Island working as a farm laborer. Evidently somewhere around that time he met a slave woman named Margaret owned by the wealthy Easton family of Portsmouth and Middletown. They fell in love and became man and wife, although due to Margaret status as a slave no marriage was recorded. They had at least two children together, John and Phebe, and those children, due to the staggered state of Rhode Island's legal path towards the end of slavery, were born free. The 1810 census of Portsmouth shows Newport Philips as a free black head of household with two other family members, those two individuals, most likely, were John and Phebe. By 1820, the slave Margaret shows up in Portsmouth as the head of household with the children under her care. Newport was back in North Kingstown at that juncture in time, working again as a farm laborer, saving money, socking it away, planning something extraordinary. You see on April 1st, 1824 Newport Philips, a free black man, made his way to Middletown with his money and his writ of manumission in hand. He went there to buy his wife of more than two decades. The results of that transaction were recorded in the town ledgers of Middletown just as his manumission had been recorded here in Wickford some 35 years earlier. Newport and Margaret Philips both left Middletown on that day free. What a glory day that must have been.

This remarkable couple disappears from the record at this point; I don't know when or where they breathed their last breathes, although I expect it was either North Kingstown or Portsmouth. Their son John stayed on in Portsmouth and married Patience Sherman. They had at least one child, James, together and John, who worked his whole life as a farmhand, died in 1876. Their son James lived in Newport as an adult, had a wife named Louise and was a fisherman until the end of his days. Newport and Margaret's daughter Phebe eventually married Daniel N. Morse, a sexton at the Methodist Episcopal Church in Providence's second ward. They had children together and she died in 1871. The slave Newport Philips lives on through the heirs of his children and grand children where ever they may be.

The old Philips family graveyard can be found in the midst of the Haverhill neighborhood off of Tower Hill Road on land that was once part of the vast family holdings; in it stand a number of fine gravestones of this important family. The slave graveyard of those same Philips is lost as of now; it was last seen in the 1950s and was noted to include 17 graves, the two named of them, Lonnon's and Hagar's, were inscribed forever with the phrase "servant of Christopher Philips". Lonnon could have been Newport's father or Hagar could have been his mother. Newport and Margaret may well be buried here or perhaps under a similar unmarked stone in Portsmouth. Where ever they are is of no real consequence I guess; what matters is that they are together and forever free.

Captives at Cocumscussoc: From Bondage to Freedom

BY NEIL DUNAY*

E very discussion of the early history of North Kingstown must begin at one place: Cocumscussoc, also known as Smith's Castle. African American history in North Kingstown certainly starts there, too. Cocumscussoc is a microcosm of Rhode Island's larger story of the enslavement of Africans and their later emancipation. From the mid-17th century to the mid-18th century, the Smith family and its heirs, the Updikes, transformed a trading house into a plantation spanning thousands of acres that surrounded the port village of Wickford that they created. Cocumscussoc was one of Rhode Island's earliest homes to enslaved Africans, and by the 1750s it held one of the largest slave populations of any plantation in the colony. Documents relating to the site shed light on the intertwined lives of both "master" and "slave," and architecture and archaeology of the site's material culture inform of us of how they lived together and apart.

To understand how slavery began here so early and so intensively, the first part of this story follows the Smith-Updike family's involvement with the institution of slavery and ownership of slaves over the first four generations in America. The second part of this narrative focuses more particularly on the stories of individual slaves living at Cocumscussoc in the second half of the eighteenth century.

Part I: Smith-Updike Family's Involvement with Slavery, 1638-1757
Richard Smith Sr (1596-1666)

Richard Smith first settled in Taunton (Cohanet) in Plymouth Colony by 1638. About the same year he set up a trading post on land the Narragansett called Cocumscussoc. Located on Wickford's North Cove, he built what Roger Williams called the "first English house" in the Narragansett country. Smith hired overseers to live at the trading house while he obtained and ferried goods back and forth on his sloop *Welcome*. Smith himself transplanted his family several times, moving first to Aquidneck Island by 1640, and then establishing a new settlement called Mespath in present day Queens on Long Island in 1642. The venture there was short-lived, as the settlers were attacked during a Dutch war with the native Wappinger tribe in 1643, and the Smith family took refuge with the Dutch on Manhattan. Smith moved back to Rhode Island about 1648, and settled permanently at Cocumscussoc where he lived until his death in 1666. No documentary evidence proves that Smith himself owned slaves, but that possibility can't be ruled out. The next generation's involvement with slavery, however, is unequivocal. [1]

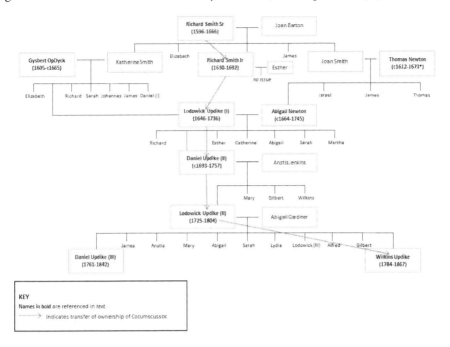

Gysbert OpDyck (1605-c1665)

While in New Amsterdam, the Smith family met a Dutch West India Company official name Gysbert Op den Dyck, his last name abbreviated OpDyck and anglicized to Updike. OpDyck married Smith's daughter, Catherine, in 1643.

The first historical record of the Smith-Updike family's involvement with a slave is tragic. In November 1639, Dutch records note the following:

> *At the requisition of the Attorney General, it was declared by Gysbert Opdyck, Commissary in Fort Hope, that he gave his black boy, named Louis Barbese the pan to fry cakes, and whereas the fire was too hot for the boy, so Opdyck took the pan in his own hand, and placed his knife in the hands of the black, then he commanded the boy to fetch a dish, who brought one very unclean, on which Opdyck struck the black, who, to evade it, tried to take hold of Opdyck, who thrusted him away, so that the boy fell down on his left side, when he kicked him with his feet. The boy then went out of the door and fell down; when Opdyck discovered the knife, crooked as a hoop, and went to look at the boy, who was wounded in his body under the left arm, **and died very suddenly.** [2]*

The Dutch "Fort de Goede hoop" was located on the Connecticut River in the southern part of today's Hartford, Connecticut. As the company's commissary, OpDyck oversaw the work of enslaved Africans. This passage is the first reference to an African American in Connecticut historical documents. At best, the passage described involuntary manslaughter, yet no subsequent records suggest that OpDyck was punished or reprimanded for his actions; in fact, he continued in the employ of the Dutch West India Company in a number of roles for nearly 25 more years. Early in the history of New Netherlands typically slaves were owned by the Dutch West India Company rather than by individuals, but the description of Louis as "*his* black boy" ("sijn Swarte Jongen") means we can't rule out that he may in fact have been owned by OpDyck. The use of the word "boy" is not pejorative; enslaved African males under the age of 16 were often employed as kitchen help, household servants, and tavern workers. The passage also provides insight into Dutch slave-naming conventions. *Barbosse* in the Dutch manuscript and *Barbese* in the translation above refers to *Berbice*, a Dutch colony located in present-day Guyana from which Louis is thought to have been imported. His original African homeland is unknown.

Following their marriage in 1643, Gysbert and Catherine (Smith) OpDyck had seven children through the year 1658. As early as June 1659, quite likely after his wife Catherine died, OpDyck moved his children to Richard Smith's house at Cocumscussoc. In a census of the inhabitants of Wickford in 1663 we find the elderly Richard Smith with a household of eight children, and no doubt seven of them were his Updike grandchildren. After filing a lawsuit in Manhattan in 1663, OpDyck's name disappears from known records. Several histories speculate he moved to Wickford permanently in 1664, where he died shortly thereafter. If OpDyck did move to Cocumscussoc and he did own slaves, it is possible he may have brought them with him to Richard Smith's household. [3]

Thomas Newton (c1612-1673?)

The story of the family's involvement with slavery moves from Gysbert OpDyck to another of Smith's sons-in-law, Thomas Newton. One of the founders of the town of Fairfield (Uncoway), Connecticut, in 1639, Newton in April 1648, then a widower, married Joan Smith without consent of the bride's parents, Richard and Joan Smith, in Dutch territory. The marriage was nullified, the sheriff who performed the ceremony was fined and dismissed, and the couple was remarried after proper proclamations of the marriage banns. In 1649, Newton further abandoned proper societal norms by engaging in an adulterous affair, then a capital offense. Newton was arrested but broke out of jail and was given sanctuary by the Smiths in Rhode Island. Knowing that Newton was within reach of British authorities, the Smiths sent the Newton family to Dutch territory on Long Island to their former Mespath lands (then called Middleburg or Newtown). From the time of their marriage to about 1664, Thomas and Joan Newton had at least four children, the last a daughter named Abigail. English officials repeatedly asked Dutch authorities to hand over the fugitive, but he remained safe until the Dutch surrendered New Netherlands to the English in 1664. Quite likely following the birth of his last child, the death of his wife, and the encroachment of English authorities, Newton decided to flee again. [4]

The documentation is now murky, but several family genealogies speculate that Newton chose Barbados as his new home, citing letters written by a Thomas Newton there in 1665 and 1666. One of his sons living in Connecticut testified in 1683 that his father died before that year. In fact a Thomas Newton does appear in Barbados probate records as having died in 1673. Barbados was home to a large and prominent Newton family, though genealogies have failed to link Thomas to this group. Might Thomas Newton have fled to an island filled with Newtons as an attempt at camouflage, a wolf in sheep's clothing? More research is needed, but given several family links to Barbados described below, Newton's residence there is quite likely. [5]

Updike family lore certainly places Newton in the Caribbean, and his trade there is of particular note:

> Thomas Newton went Cap[t] of a ship to Africa. On his return with four-hundred slaves he was shipwrecked on the Island of St. Vincent. The Slaves took possession of the Island. [They were] the first that peopled the Island of St. Vincent. [6]

Thus, members of the Smith-Updike family not only may have owned slaves, but also abetted in their kidnapping and transport, and they profited from it.

Meanwhile, Richard Smith Jr, Newton's brother-in-law, had trade business in Barbados. In 1671, he writes to John Winthrop Jr that he has been fitting out his ship to sail to Barbados. Was Smith's contact there Thomas Newton? And was Smith bringing human cargo back to Rhode Island, either for sale or for his own household?

Further supporting Newton's residence on Barbados is an entry in a passenger list. From Barbados on 15 July 1679, Abigail Newton boarded the ship *Eliza* for Boston. Had daughter Abigail been living in Barbados with her father? Once in Boston, Abigail Newton would have been close to Cocumscussoc, where several of her brothers had inherited estates from Richard Smith and where her Updike cousins were living. Abigail Newton appears in Wickford as witness on a deed, next to her first cousin Lodowick Updike, in May 1687. Perhaps not coincidentally, the deed she witnessed was sale of land by her uncle Richard Smith Jr to gunsmith William Palmer, "late ye Island of Barbados." Abigail Newton married Lodowick Updike by 1691, and the Updike-Newton lines of the Smith family converged. [7]

Richard Smith Jr (1630-1692)

When Richard Smith left New Amsterdam in the late 1640s to settle permanently in Rhode Island, he left his youngest son, Richard Jr, then about age 19, to continue his business there. During the 1650s the younger Smith likely moved goods back and forth between Manhattan and Cocumscussoc, as his name appears frequently in deeds around Wickford during the period, but he is mentioned in connection with a house in Manhattan in 1661. The 1660 Castello Plan of New Amsterdam depicts the Smith family's holdings, located on Hoogh Straet (High Street and today Stone Street). Notably, the Smith house was located not far from the Dutch West India Company's slave quarters, about a block away on Slyck Steegh ("Dirty Lane"), which paralleled Hoogh Straet. [8]

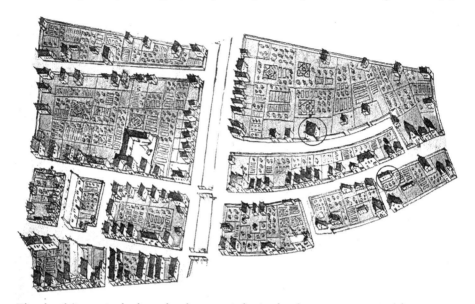

The building circled at the lower right is the house occupied by Richard Smith Jr (the Smiths at one time owned the entire block). The building circled above and to the left of Smith's house is the slave quarters of the Dutch West India Company.

As a young businessman, Smith Jr must have been fascinated with the Dutch operations and soaked up as much as he could possibly learn from them. He would have seen how the Dutch had imported slaves and used them to advance the Dutch West India Company's trading empire. The young Richard Smith would have wanted to emulate the Dutch elite, not only with their stylish houses and furniture, fancy imported porcelain, and new tea traditions, but also their use of slaves in both home and business.

By the end of 1662, the Smiths had sold their house and storehouse in Manhattan, as well as adjacent lots they owned, suggesting Richard Smith Jr had moved back to Cocumscussoc by then. When Smith Jr returned to Cocumscussoc, the family business was in jeopardy. Beaver, the one trade item that had lifted the Smith family into New England's super-wealthy elite, was nearly extinct in Rhode Island. As modern MBAs might say, Smith needed a new business model. Inheriting his father's trading business and the bulk of his lands at Cocumscussoc (and elsewhere) in 1666, Smith Jr could begin the transition. Smith would transform Cocumscussoc from a trading post to a farming enterprise that would supply plantations in the Caribbean. The fertile land around Wickford could support small crops of wheat, corn, flax, and even tobacco, but Smith eventually realized that meat and dairy were the sweet spot. By 1675, Smith had accumulated more than 26 head of cattle, 30 hogs, and 100 goats. By 1692, he had 135 cattle, 30 sheep, and 20 hogs, showing the specialization of his business toward cheese made from cow's milk. His references to Barbados in letters to John Winthrop Jr indicate one of his target markets, though he supplied closer markets as well. Slave labor became an instrumental part of his operation. [9]

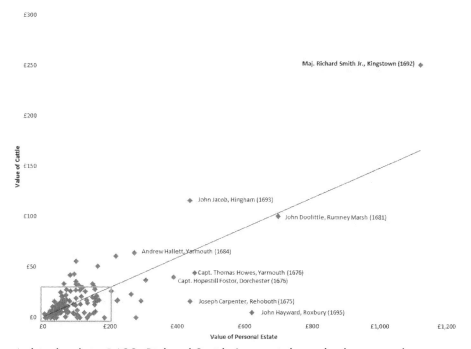

At his death in 1692, Richard Smith Jr certainly ranked among the wealthiest men in New England. This chart compares total personal estate values versus cattle for 120 probate inventories in Plymouth County and rural Suffolk County, Massachusetts, 1675-1699. (Unfortunately Rhode Island probate inventories have not been adequately transcribed or published for comparison.) Of the 120 inventories, 86 percent had a total personal estate value of less than £200 and 86 percent had a value for cattle of less than £30. The box at lower left defines this group. The diagonal line shows the average ratio of cattle to total personal estate value. The value of Richard Smith's estate, both in total and in cattle, far exceeds the values of other inventories. Smith's estate also had a higher ratio of cattle to total inventory than other estate inventories, demonstrating his intensive investment in his dairy operation. Only five of the other 120 estate inventories listed any slaves; the highest total slave value of those five was £25 versus £80 for Richard Smith.

Caesar, Sarah, and Ebed-Melich

In his will dated 16 March 1690/1, Richard Smith Jr directed the following: *I give unto my negro **Caesar** and to **his wife Sarah**, their freedom after my decease and one hundred acres of land in convenient place, to be laid out by Lodowick Updike on some of my outshares of land either mortgage or surplusage of the neck. Also I give unto **Caesar's children** all their freedom when thirty years old and to **Ebed-melich** the like freedom, and the land Caesar is to have to him and his heirs forever, this after my wife's decease, not in her life time, for she shall possess her life in all.*

Following Smith's death a little more than a year later, an inventory of his estate was taken on 3 May 1692. It lists:

two negro men Cost   £40   00
five negro Children & an old negro Woman £40   00

Piecing together the two documents, the two men listed in the inventory are Caesar and Ebed-Melich, the old woman is Sarah, and the five children are those of Caesar and Sarah. The fact that Sarah is described as old and that this family exists as a unit suggests that Caesar and Sarah have been with the Smiths for years, perhaps decades. It would be quite rare for an entire family to be purchased as slaves and kept together. More likely, Caesar and Sarah were purchased separately when much younger and brought back to Cocumscussoc where they met, ultimately wed, and had children. To be described as old, Sarah must have been at least 40 when the inventory was taken, suggesting a birth date no later than 1652. In 1671, when Smith was trading with Barbados, Sarah would have been of desirable age to a slave buyer like Smith.

The inventory pinpoints where in the house the slaves were quartered:

In ye Kitchen Garrett Servants Beds & Covering £03   00

While in the southern colonies slaves were often quartered in housing separate from the main house, in Rhode Island slaves typically lived in the main house with the family. Garrets (attics) were commonly chosen spaces to keep the captives. Based on the room names in the inventory and the architecture of the remodeled but extant house, we can pinpoint the location of this room (see figure).

This attic room now looks very different from 1678 due to a remodeling of the house's roofline about 1738 and subsequent renovations and restorations over the centuries. Yet, even today it gives us an idea about the conditions that Caesar, Sarah and their family endured. The space is stifling hot in summer and freezing in winter. Windows were small, the ceilings were low and slanted, and there were no fireplaces. We can imagine a scene in deep winter as the family huddled against the central chimney to latch onto whatever warmth it radiated from the fireplaces in the rooms below. Yet, the family probably welcomed their time in this space, alone and unobserved by the

Kitchen Garrett

Kitchen Chamber

Kitchen

Per Smith's 1692 estate inventory, the servant quarters were in the "Kitchen Garrett," a space likely occupied by Caesar, Sarah, and their five children, possibly as well as Ebed-Melich.

Smith family, when they were able to share time together as a family, and they could privately practice their African traditions and religion.

Despite the renovations, the floor in this room today may still be the same as in 1692. This is important, as under the attic floor in another Rhode Island house of this period, Newport's Wanton-Lyman-Hazard house (c1697), was discovered a cache of objects believed to have been hidden by slaves. The stash was a bundle of cloth which contained objects like nails, pits, beads, pins, corncobs, and a cowrie shell. Historians believe these are *minkisi*, objects hidden in households along the African coast around the Kongo area, to ward off evil spirits. [10]

To date at the Smith house no one has pried up these attic boards to see what (if anything) they may conceal. But objects were discovered secreted away in the walls of a room two stories below this attic space. John Hutchins Cady, who restored the house into the "Smith's Castle" museum in the 1950s to early 1960s, discovered a group of objects in the west wall of the room that served as the Smith's kitchen. The objects, which appear to date from the mid-18th century (therefore later than Caesar and Sarah's residence), included various household objects: shoe-buckles, eating utensils, horseshoe fragments, and a book. Also among these domestic objects appeared Native American lithics, stone tools made in the remote past. Archaeological investigations of African-American sites, particularly in the South, have yielded evidence that Africans collected Native American lithics that they likely discovered while working the fields. Ethno-historians believe they used them as "power objects" in magical practices or religious rituals. Their occurrence is also documented in the North, as recently a similar item was discovered under the floor of the slave quarters at the Royall house in Medford, Massachusetts.

In a world in which enslaved people had little control over their daily lives, charms and associated potions and incantations instilled feelings of safety and protection and offered a way for them to seemingly manage their destiny. [11]

In 1951, John Hutchins Cady, the architect who restored the Smith-Updike house into the "Smith's Castle" house museum, displays "implements found back of lathe in west wall" in the room used by the Smiths as a kitchen.

We Were Here Too

Cady's cache assemblage as photographed in 2013 shows the lithic, a projectile point, circled at the lower left. Comparison of the original photo with the 2013 box suggests some items, possibly lithics, are now missing from the original discovery.

Despite Smith's promise of freedom and disbursement of land to Caesar and Sarah, the fragmented remaining land records of the Town of North Kingstown offer no proof that the promise was kept. We do have evidence, however, that Ebed-Melich obtained his freedom. In Supreme Court records, we find the following entry:

> *Melich a Negroe Man of North Kingstown ... 16th of July 1724 ...*
> *[against] Samuel Rhodes.*
> *[Marginal note:] Judgment satisfied by Rhodes to Daniel Updike att. to Melich Negroe. [12]*

The entry is interesting: Ebed-Melich had legal status to sue in court, and he won (or favorably settled) his case. All the more striking is that he was represented by a member of his former captor's family, Daniel Updike, who then (1724) was the sitting attorney general of the colony! After this, Ebed-Melich disappears from the record.

Daniel Updike (c1694-1757)
When Richard Smith Jr died in 1692, he left the bulk of his estate to his nephew, Lodowick Updike, who had recently married his first cousin, Abigail Newton. Thus, not only did the Smith-Newton-Updike blood line converge

with this couple's marriage, but so did the vast Smith financial empire. In turn, Lodowick and Abigail's son, Daniel, was the key beneficiary, and he greatly expanded the family's involvement with slavery. [13]

About 1715, when Daniel Updike was about 21, he followed the paths of others in his family and took a trip to Barbados. One of his descendants, Wilkins Updike, wrote:

> *After Daniel's education was completed, he visited Barbados, in the company of a friend of his father's; and was admitted to the first circles of society on the Island. [14]*

The friend of his father was likely John Chace, Updike's future brother-in-law, whose family owned plantations on Barbados. If Thomas Newton was in fact related to the Newtons on Barbados, we can imagine Daniel visiting them as well. Like Richard Smith Jr in New Amsterdam, Daniel Updike on Barbados as a young man would have been keenly interested in how the planters organized the plantations and how they best employed their slave labor. The reference to "the first circles of society" gives us the impression that Daniel was visiting the plantation houses of fine families, sitting in elegant parlors drinking tea, and making proper connections with all the right people. While these scenarios likely occurred, Daniel Updike was probably also involved in some less refined activities. A modern "spring break" might be a more apt description. [15]

John Greenwood's c1755 depiction of Rhode Island "sea captains carousing in Surinam" shows how slave traders occupied themselves in foreign ports. (John Greenwood, American, 1727–1792; Sea Captains Carousing in Surinam, c. 1752-58; oil on bed ticking; 37 3/4 x 75 inches; Saint Louis Art Museum, Museum Purchase 256:1948.)

Though created about forty years after Updike's trip, this painting, called "Sea Captains carousing in Surinam," may give a hint as to the other activities Updike enjoyed on Barbados. The scene shows the Rhode Island sea captains, many of whom were involved in the slave trade, celebrating in a tavern. The description by the Saint Louis Art Museum notes, "[Artist] John Greenwood presents a humorous scene in which intoxicated men dance, smoke, cheat at cards, spill their drink, fall asleep, and even vomit from their overindulgence." For some the scene might not be so humorous. Note the African servants depicted, particularly the diminutive figure in the lower right, a young boy much like Louis Barbese, enslaved under-age labor.

While this painting does not depict Updike himself, it comes quite close to him. Four of the figures depicted at the table are known prominent Rhode Island political figures. The sorriest looking one — the man slumped in his chair, wig off his head, passed out, and being "doused with punch and vomit" — would later become a governor of Rhode Island. He is Joseph Wanton, and he was Daniel Updike's step-son. So when we talk about what Wilkins Updike called the "first circles of society," these are the Rhode Islanders who were in Updike's first circle, the perpetuators and beneficiaries of the institution of slavery. [16]

After returning from Barbados, Daniel Updike married into the Arnold family, an important political dynasty, in 1717, thus boosting his own political ambitions. In 1722, when he was not even yet a freeman himself, he was elected as the colony's attorney general, a position he would hold until 1732 and again from 1741 until his death in 1757. He was the longest serving attorney general in Rhode Island history. [17]

One of Updike's first assignments from the general assembly put him at the center of Rhode Island's slavery institution:

> 1723 June 18 — Voted, that Mr. Daniel Updike, the attorney general, be and he hereby is ordered, appointed and empowered to gather in the money due to this colony, for the importation of negroes, and to prosecute, sue and implead such person or persons as shall refuse to pay the same; and that he be allowed five shillings per head, for every slave that shall be hereafter imported into this colony, out of the impost money; and that he be also allowed ten per cent. more for all such money as he shall recover of the outstanding debts; and in all respects to have the like power as was given to the naval officer by the former act. [18]

Updike would have become quite wealthy from the general import of slaves into the colony as well as from recovering unpaid taxes on the same owed to colony. It's not known how long this arrangement lasted. We might even surmise that in this barter economy, some payments to Updike were made with goods, even with slaves. That might partly explain the large increase in the number of slaves at Cocumscussoc from the time of his father's death 1737 to his own death in 1757.

Part II: Enslaved and Free African-Americans at Cocumscussoc, 1757-1824.

Snapshot: The Updike Household in 1757
At his death in 1737, Lodowick Updike owned at least one slave, named Penny Time, and probably one or a few more. By 1757, Daniel Updike at his death owned "18 Negros" who are listed by name and value in his probate inventory taking 5 June 1757:

Nathaniel Vallewed at nothing	
Charles	*£ 300*
Moses	*600*
Joseph	*600*
Dimas	*600*
Newport	*500*
Dublin	*600*
Mingo	*450*
Claro	*400*
James	*400*
Cæsar	*200*
Dominic at Nothing	
Paul 2 Years Old	*100*
Prince	*50*
Sue	*100*
Lille and Child	*500*
Bridget	*250*
Robie 2½ Years Old	*100*

As with Smith's probate inventory of 1692, Updike's probate inventory gives us a view into this household in 1757. A probate inventory is an itemization of the deceased's personal estate, used to assess probate taxes. During this period, inventories were taken by fellow citizens, quite frequently neighbors. Their task was to move room by room, itemizing the contents of each room, and assigning a value to each item. Slaves, if any, were then itemized, and then following the slaves the livestock were valued. The document underscores the status of slaves as personal possessions and of little more consequence than the cattle, hogs, and sheep.

Imagine the scene as the 18 slaves at Cocumscussoc are gathered together, perhaps at the back of the house, and lined up for inspection. The inventory-takers examine the men, women, and children one by one, perhaps looking into their mouths (and elsewhere) to assess their health, and then assign a value to each human life. They value the elderly, like Nathaniel and Dominic, at very little or even "at nothing." To healthy males in their late teens and twenties, like Moses, Joseph, Dimas, and Dublin, they assign the highest values. They assign lower values to women than to men. To these 18 humans, the inventory-takers assign a sum value of £5,750, 44 percent of Daniel Updike's personal wealth. Today that is the equivalent of $1.2 million. [19]

The probate inventory also gives us clues about the daily lives of the people

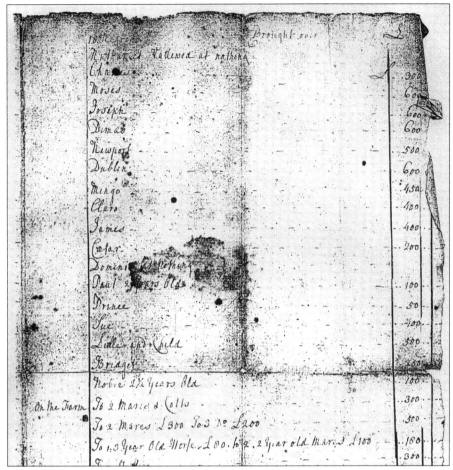

Daniel Updike's 1757 estate inventory lists "18 Negroes" right after the room-by-room listing of personal possessions and right before the livestock. The inventory takers valued the captives at nearly half of Updike's entire personal estate.

held captive by the Updikes. A large, long room at the rear of the house holds a massive brick fireplace with two beehive ovens on the back wall. In 1757 this room was called the backroom, and it functioned as the Updike's kitchen. Today museum visitors guided by an elderly white female docent in period costume are presented a Colonial-Revival impression of the room, like a Wallace Nutting photo. These artsy products of early 20th century imagination, in sepia with water-color highlights, typically show one or two white women, dressed in fine colonial clothing, sitting in rocking chairs, and performing some light domestic household chores, like knitting or needlework. All is tranquil, peaceful, and calm. The photos present a nostalgic, idealized image that almost exclaim, "Those were the good old days!"

Daniel Updike's backroom, the hub of activity in the 1757 household, as photographed in the Smith's Castle house museum about 2004.

The reality of Updike's backroom was quite different, the probate inventory tells us. Rather than the peaceful domain of the mistress, it was the hectic sweat shop for the enslaved laborers, the bustling hub of the Updike household. In this room we find the following items, arranged by type of activity:

Cooking	Spinning	Farming	Serving
andirons	3 spinning wheels	6 axes	18 plates
4 kettles	2 hetchels	5 hoes	15 pewter dishes
3 iron pots	various yarns	4 sickles	7 brass candlesticks
3 skillets		3 plows	6 towels
pickle pot		auger	6 napkins
coffee mill		cooper tools	3 tablecloths
warming pan		saddle	

In the backroom, cooking was the principal occupation, a strenuous and dangerous task. Counting the members of the Updike family, the 18 slaves, several indentured servants, and an unknown number of visitors stopping in at any time off the busy Post Road, the African-American women were cooking multiple meals for at least 30 people every day. They repeatedly lugged up, down, and over, huge and heavy iron pots. The fire smoked their eyes. The women were always at risk of either catching their skirts on fire or (more likely) burning themselves on the searing iron cookware, creating sores that could lead to infection.

We Were Here Too

But cooking wasn't their only assignment. The three spinning wheels beckoned. The women were no doubt were given quotas for turning fleece into wool and flax into linen yarns. They were on double-duty, spinning yarn while making sure the meals didn't burn. Were they also making soap? Dipping candles? Washing laundry? The chores in this huge household were never done.

Here we also find the farm tools. We can imagine the male slaves coming in from the fields and pastures at the end of the day, dropping their tools on the floor of the backroom before they get their evening meal. The tools are there ready for them the next day when the tiresome, back-breaking routine starts again.

Finally, this room contains the objects needed to serve the household. Note that while we find pewter, brass, and cloth objects, we don't see fine china or silver. The latter was kept locked away in the fanciest rooms, the key kept by the mistress of the house securely on a chain at her waist or secreted in her pocket. But the enslaved were present in those elegant rooms, too. They served the family and their distinguished visitors. Architecture, furniture, china, silver, clothing, and servant all proclaimed to any visitor the social status of the occupants of this house.

Enslaved people worked not only in the kitchen and fields but in every space of the house. The John Potter family of Matunuck is being served in their parlor by their engaging enslaved young boy. He means little more to them than any other possession, a sign of their wealth and social status, occupying the same plane in the painting as the Potters' clothing, table, and tea service. (Unknown artist; Overmantle of the Potter Family, Rhode Island c. 1740; oil on wood; Gift of Mrs. E.L. Winters, Newport Historical Society 53.3.)

In Rhode Island, one of the most elegant and succinct expressions of this "need to impress" is the c1740 painted overmantle from the John Potter house in Matunuck, now in the collections of the Newport Historical Society. The Potters not only wanted to affirm their elevated social status through their possessions, they wanted to preserve the moment for all posterity.

To some viewers the inclusion of the house boy in the portrait meant that the Potters considered him one of the family. The reality is quite the opposite. The painting can be divided in half by a line drawn horizontally. Everyone above the line is family, everything below are their possessions. You can almost hear each of the family members boasting about their cosmopolitan tastes:

Our new tea set finally arrived from China!

I commissioned this tea table from the Goddard shop in Newport, and it is made from the finest mahogany imported from the West Indies!

Oh, this dress? Well, it's silk and I custom-ordered it from London, where it is the best and current fashion!

and

We just imported our boy from Barbados, and we can't do without him!

But in this case, in this time period, it is more likely that this boy in the Potter house was born on the farm, born into slavery, and this is the only life he has ever known.

***

In addition to general ideas about what slaves were doing in the Updike household and where, we can also glean some biographical details for a few of the enslaved laborers listed in Updike's probate inventory.

Mingo (bef. 1723-aft.1757)

While in the household of Richard Smith Jr, Caesar and Sarah, at least for a time, could stay together and raise a family of five children, but other enslaved families were not so fortunate. As an enslaved person, marrying and forming a family was difficult at best, and families could be torn apart by the master on a whim. Mingo's predicament is an example.

In the 1757 probate inventory, Mingo's assigned value relative to other males (£450) suggests that he was not in his prime but still fit enough to work. Mingo makes an anonymous appearance 14 years earlier in a diary kept by Rev. James MacSparran, the rector of St. Paul's Church, a close friend of the Updike family and a frequent visitor to Cocumscussoc:

[1743] October 24. This morning my negro woman Maroca was bro't to bed of another Girl. Good God do thou direct me what to do with her. I am Perplexed about her Conduct with Col. Updike's negro. She is a Christian, but seems not concerned about her soul, nor minds her promise of chastity, which she has often made me.

Two years later, the name of Updike's slave and the father of Maroca's child, is revealed:

> *[1745] June 25ᵗʰ Harry hilling Corn. I bled George Fowler and [gave] Maroca one or two Lashes for receiving Presents from Mingo. I think it was my Duty to correct her, and we'ever Passion passed between my wife and me on yˢ occasion, Good Lᵈ forgive it. [20]*

From the first text, we see that Maroca has given birth to a daughter, and this wasn't the only child she gave birth to in MacSparran's household. MacSparran's reaction to Maroca's continued efforts to build a family with Mingo was violence. MacSparran's complicated relationship with his slaves has been discussed by several scholars. [21] The focus of our subject is Mingo, but all we are left with are questions. What kind of position did Mingo hold in the Updike household that he was able to travel to the MacSparran house and meet secretly with Maroca and on multiple occasions? Certainly the Updikes placed a great deal of trust in Mingo.

Documents fail to shed light on what happened to Mingo, Maroca, and their children after Updike's and MacSparran's deaths (which both occurred in 1757). The family disappears from written records in Rhode Island. One hopes they eventually were able to come together as a family, but certainly they faced great odds in doing so.

Prince Updike (1711-1781)

Unlike Mingo, in 1757 Prince seemed to be at the end of his useful life as a slave, valued at only £50. Later documents reveal, however, that his productive life was not over. Although the means are uncertain, Prince appears to have obtained his freedom shortly after Daniel Updike's death. By 1766 he appears in Newport working for the merchant Aaron Lopez in an unusual capacity. Heading one of the pages of the Lopez account book we find "Negro Prince Updike, Chocolate Grinder."

> *Lopez delivered raw cocoa to Updike and Updike returned ground chocolate for which he received five shillings for every pound prepared. Between 1766 and 1767, Updike produced 2000 pounds of chocolate from 2500 pounds of cocoa, and between 1768 and 1769, Updike produce 4000 pounds of ground chocolate from 5000 pounds of cocoa. [22]*

In the eighteenth century, chocolate drinking was a fashionable trend and a highly demanded product in Europe. Americans were exporting tons of ground cocoa to support the fad.

The process of grinding cacao was difficult work. Prince Updike didn't have the convenience of a device similar to a coffee mill, with a comfortable handle on a wheel that he simply turned round and round. Cacao grinding involved kneeling in front of a small crude stone platform (called a *metate*) with a stone rolling pin (*mano*), first breaking and removing the husks around the cacao and then repeatedly rolling the *mano* over the cacao to produce the desired fineness of grind.

"When ye man goeth to break the cacao & take of ye husks he kneeleth thus." This image of a chocolate grinder from the journal of the first Earl of Sandwich, c1668, shows how the grinder knelt at the stone metate to roll the mano over the cacao beans. See Kate Loveman, "The Introduction of Chocolate into England: Retailers, Researchers, and Consumers, 1640–1730," Journal of Social History 47:1 (Fall 2013), 27-46.

Given the amount of cacao produced and price paid, Prince Updike would have made £1,500 over the four years the account books record. In today's money, that is about $300,000, a sum that must have seemed unfathomable to the former slave.

We find proof of Prince Updike's wealth upon his death in January 1781 at age 70. Buried in "God's Little Acre," the African section of the Newport Common Burying Ground, his grave is marked by an expensive and elegant stone carved at the famous Stevens stone shop in Newport, and as indicated by the initials J.S. at the bottom, carved by John Stevens, the master stone mason.

Dimas [Smith?] (bef.1737-aft. 1791)

While Prince Updike may have found a legal path to freedom, some enslaved people opted for another route: running away. Dimas, one of the most valuable slaves in the 1757 probate inventory, appears to have done just that. Lodowick Updike II (1725-1804), the heir to Daniel Updike's

When he died at age 70 in 1781, Prince Updike had to have a considerable amount of money to afford this elegant headstone, carved at the John Stevens shop by the master himself, as indicated by the initials J.S. at the bottom of the stone. He is buried in "God's Little Acre," the African cemetery within the Newport Common Burying Ground. (Photo by Barb Austin Courtesy the Rhode Island Genealogical Society)

estate, which included his slaves, placed the following advertisement in the *Providence Gazette* on April 30, 1763:

> RUN *away from the Subscriber at North-Kingstown, in the Colony of Rhode-Island, a young Negro Man named Dimas, born in this Country, a well set Fellow about 5 Feet 4 Inches high, has a down Look, is thin jaw'd, and has a visible Scar from the Bridge of his Nose, over his Cheek, reaching beyond the Corner of his Mouth. He had on when he went off, a new double-breasted Jacket of Snuff colour'd Broad-cloth, trim'd with Horn Buttons, and Breeches of the same; he wore a low brim'd Hat, and affects of the Sailor. He is a subtil Fellow, and has got a forged Pass, with which it is suspected he will effect his Escape to Boston, as he has some Acquaintances there. Whoever takes up said Fellow, and delivers him to me, or secures him so that I may get him again, shall be intitled to SIX DOLLARS Reward, and have all reasonable charge, paid. LODOWICK UPDIKE. [23]*

The ad provides great detail about Dimas. We learn he was born "in this Country," most likely at Cocumscussoc. He was a slave in Rhode Island, yet he had acquaintances in Boston. He wore new clothes; were they provided by the Updikes, or stolen as part of his get-away? Most telling, he had a long scar across his face. Did this result from the brutality of the work … or that of the master? Dimas apparently was caught and ran away again in 1767. [24]

Subsequent records show Dimas returned to the farm yet again. Daniel Updike III (1761-1842), son of Lodowick and grandson of Daniel, kept daybooks for the Updike farms in the 1790s. He noted:

> *Dimas (the son of Robi Smith) came here to live [as] a volunteer April 1st 1791. [25]*

A volunteer is a former slave who, although free, returns to the farm to live and work as he or she had before, receiving simple room and board and no wages. Sadly, this option was a last resort for elderly freed African Americans who had no viable means of making a living. One interesting point is that Dimas is called the son of Robi Smith (so was he Dimas Smith?), which suggests perhaps that he (and perhaps Robi) descended from Caesar and Sarah, the couple enslaved by Richard Smith Jr.

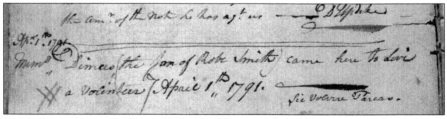

In his farm journal, Daniel Updike III notes that Dimas came back to the farm to work as a volunteer, an unpaid laborer. Through Updike's eyes, the event was a proper twist of fate for a slave that once (or twice) tried to run away.

We can conclude that this Dimas is the same as the run-away by a sarcastic remark made by Daniel Updike at the end of the entry. Daniel Updike can't resist noting the irony …

Sic Volvere Parcas

The Latin, from Virgil's *Aeneid*, means literally "thus to turn the fates around" or more simply "so turns fate" – an apropos comment for someone who tried to escape their fate as a slave (as perceived by Updike) only to come full circle and return to this fate of his own volition.

James Updike (bef.1750-1829)

In 1784, Rhode Island passed the Gradual Emancipation Act, which allowed slave owners to free slaves between the ages of 21 and 40 without incurring any financial responsibility for them. The Revolutionary War crippled the Rhode Island economy and many key export markets were no longer accessible. Struggling economically, many plantation owners took advantage of the law and freed their slaves.

It appears Lodowick Updike began freeing his slaves much earlier. From 18 slaves in 1757, the Updike household included 11 blacks (presumably all slaves) listed in the 1774 census. The 1777 military census listed just four blacks in the Updike household, and by 1790 there were four free non-whites but only three slaves. By 1800, just one free non-white and two slaves remained, and by 1810 the household had only one non-white resident. [26]

James Updike is likely one of the slaves who benefited from the 1784 law. Given his lower ascribed value in 1757, he was probably not yet a teenager when Daniel Updike died. In 1784 he may have been about thirty-five years old, and about that time he probably obtained his freedom, married, and started a family. His household is enumerated in the 1790 census as "James Updike Negro" with seven "all other free persons," that is, non-white, non-slave residents of all ages, presumably husband, wife, and five children.

North Kingstown records provide the names, though unfortunately not the birth years, for the family, including subsequent children.

> *Births of the children of James Updike alias C____ton by Freelove his Wife —- viz*
>
> *Joseph Updike born July*
> *Abby Updike born June 26th …… AD*
> *Sally Updike born December 20th ………*
> *John Updike born March 2 ………*
> *James Updike Jr born October 20th ……..*
> *Nathanial Updike born October 16th …*
> *Susanna Updike born May 9th …*
> *Celia Updike born January 10th …*
> *Lavina Updike born August 6th ..*
> *[another burned from the manuscript]*

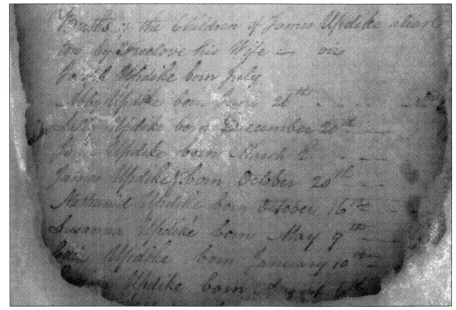

A fragmented page in North Kingstown records, with birth years burned from the margin, lists the children of James and Freelove Updike.

James N. Arnold transcribed an additional two children in this family group:
Ceasar, Oct. 3, _____
Christopher, Aug. 20, _____ [27]

The indication that James had an alias is curious; for what reason and what was it? (The surname Cranston is one that fits the blank.) To fit with the 1790 census, the first five children at least were born before 1790. Ceasar and Christopher appear in later records as crew on ships out of Wickford in the early 1820s, with their ages suggesting birth years of 1798 and 1802, respectively. Working as a sailor was one of the few options open to free blacks. It was dangerous but paid well relative to farm work. By the 1830s, it is estimated about 20 percent of all maritime workers in the United States were of African American descent. [28]

James Updike's household is not enumerated in the 1800 or 1810 censuses (either as Updike or Cranston), but reappears in 1820, in a household of three, presumably he and his wife and a daughter. James died on 22 January 1829, and his wife Freelove is enumerated as head of her own household in the 1830 census. [29]

Caesar Updike (1755-1819)
Male slaves were given a unique opportunity for gaining their freedom in 1778. In February of that year the Rhode Island General Assembly recruited slaves into a battalion to fight against the British. Slave owners were

compensated up to £120 for each slave that enlisted. Two slaves in Lodowick Updike's household took advantage of the new law and enlisted in May 1778.

Date.	Slave's Name.	Master's Name.	Value.
May 8	Moses Updike	Lodowick Updike, N.K.	£93
May 8	Ceaser Updike	Lodowick Updike, N K.	£120

Of the 38 slaves listed on this roster for South County, only four were valued at less than £100, including Moses at £93 (others were £90, £60, and £30). Moses, in his prime in 1757, was one of the highest valued slaves in Daniel Updike's household. Now twenty years later he is no longer in prime form for labor. One slave was listed at £130, which is above the ceiling established in the law (an error?). Caeser and 23 others were valued at £120. Of the listed 23 were from South Kingstown, 8 from North Kingstown, 4 from Hopkinton, 2 from Westerly, and 1 from Exeter. By June 1778, Caesar and Moses were both serving at Valley Forge under Captain Thomas Cole. [30]

At this point, Moses disappears from the records, but information on Caesar continues. The Regimental Book for the First R.I. Regiment at the Rhode Island State Archives described Caesar Updike in 1778 as: *[age] 23; 5' 5¼"; laborer; born R. Island, N. Kingston, Washington Co.; residence: N. Kingstown, Washington Co.; hair: black; complexion: Mustee. Enlisted 1778 at E. Greenwich for the War.*

The racial designation "mustee" suggests that Caesar had both African and Native American ancestry. It is likely that indentured Native Americans mixed with enslaved Africans on the Updike farm.

Image showing the uniform of a soldier from the 1st Rhode Island Regiment, c1780. Caesar Updike enlisted in 1778 and served until 1783. From Jean Baptiste Antoine de Verger, "Journal des faits les plus importants, arrivé aux troupes françaises aux ordres de Mr. le Comte de Rochambeau," 1781-1784.

On 1 May 1779, Caesar was listed as a private in Col. Christopher Greene's Rhode Island Regiment. Caesar appeared at a court martial hearing on 5 September 1779, having been previously convicted of some offense against his superior officer. The Lt. Col. reduced the punishment previously ordered, noting, "As there were circumstances of particular [cut] indecency in Corpl Staffords behaviour to Cesar Updikes Wife," he was only to receive "20 Stripes" on his naked back (the minimum punishment). He, along with many of his fellows, was furloughed at Saratoga from 22 December 1782 to 20 February 1783 by Lt. Col. Com. Olney. He served four years in the 4th company and was entitled to one Honorary Badge of Distinction. He was discharged 15 June 1783. [31]

Caesar Updike is not listed as a head of household in the 1790 census. In 1794 he appears to have applied (probably unsuccessfully) for a pension related to his military service in the amount of $338.91. As early as May 1795 and as late as April 1798, the Updike daybooks show, Caesar returned to the Updike farm to work. Unlike Dimas who "volunteered," Caesar returned as a wage laborer. In a barter economy, wages were not as we think of them today. Caesar was paid only occasionally with currency; most of his payments were made with corn. Once his "paycheck" was a pair of shoes. His activities on the farm varied with the seasons; planting, weeding, chopping wood, and mending fences are frequently listed. [32]

Caesar's household appears in the 1800 census as including seven "other free persons," not in North Kingstown but in East Greenwich. The large household suggests Caesar and his wife have had children. By 1810, he had returned to North Kingstown, where his household then comprised five people. [33]

Caesar again applied for a pension in April 1818. His statement is remarkable and poignant:

> I Caezer Updike (a man of colour) of North Kingstown in the district of Rhode Island on solemn oath do declare and say that in the month of February or March in the year 1778 I enlisted as a private soldier in Capt Micah Whitmarsh's company, Col. Christopher Greene's regiment in the continental army of the United States in the Rhode Island line in which service I continued during the war. I then received a written discharge signed by George Washington, which discharge was consumed by fire together with my house. I further declare that I am now in reduced circumstances & stand in need of the assistance of my Country for support.
>
> -----------------------
>
> his
> Caezer X Updike
> Mark

Thomas Reynolds, a neighbor in North Kingstown, wrote in support of Caesar's application:

> From my knowledge of his circumstances I now believe him to be very poor and indigent not possessing any property whatsoever — & as far as I have known him said Updike has been an industrious hard working

man, but now in consequence of his blindness I think him incapable of supporting himself.

The records indicate that Caeser received his pension, a total of $161.33 ($96 per year), but that he died on 13 December 1819. No subsequent information has been discovered about his wife or children. [34]

The Burying Ground

As in life, in death enslaved people stayed close to, yet separate from, their captors. A plat survey of the Updike farm, drawn in 1802, shows the "burying point" to the east of the house. The Smith-Updike family's cemetery, neatly enclosed and today on private property, is north of the burying point shown. And just north of the family plot, ever so near but distinctly separate, is the burial ground for their servants, mostly enslaved but perhaps also some indentured.

George Harris, who about 1883 documented the "Ancient Burial Grounds of Old Kingstowne," described it as, "on plain north of the above [Updike] yards in open lot quite an extensive burial yard of the colored servants of the above families." Harris counted 72 large and 8 small graves all with rude stones. He speculates that there may have been more whose markers have been removed. [35]

Thus, in 1883 there were at least 81 burials, and probably more, substantiating the large number of people enslaved by the Smith-Updike families. To date we have discovered the names of only 20 people who may have been buried there. Much more research remains to uncover these people's untold stories.

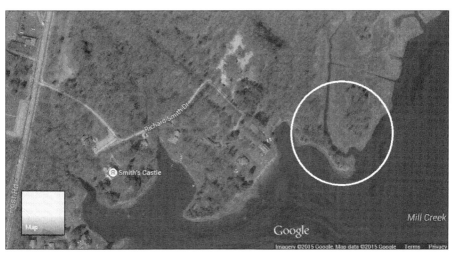

An 1802 survey of the land holdings of Lodowick Updike identified the circled area as the Burying Point. The precise location of the cemeteries, which are on private property, is intentionally not shown to preserve the integrity of the cemeteries as well as the privacy of the owners. (Image courtesy Google Earth).

*Background & Acknowledgments

This narrative is based on presentations I made at the North Kingstown Free Library in February 2012 and the East Greenwich Historic Preservation Society in January 2014. In turn, the presentations were based on about five years of research on African-Americans at Cocumscussoc as part of a plan to improve and expand the interpretation of the lives of the enslaved, not only as part of the house tour but extending across the landscape in areas formerly occupied by fields, orchards, and outbuildings. The plan was never implemented.

As people learned of my project, many researchers came forward to help by identifying documents they had discovered or pointing me in helpful directions. I am especially thankful to the following individuals:

Cherry Fletcher Bamberg, FASG
G. Timothy Cranston
Catherine DeCesare, PhD
R. Darrell McIntire
Joanne Pope Melish, PhD
Colin Porter, PhD
Patricia E. Rubertone, PhD

I am especially indebted to Tim Cranston for inviting me to contribute this information to his book. Of course any errors, omissions, and misinterpretations are mine alone.

This project has been a joy. Though they may have lived hundreds of years ago, the people whose histories I have narrated have become close friends. So much about their lives and legacies remains undiscovered, but I hope that in some small way I have given them voice.

Notes

1. In testimony given in July 1679, John Greene of Quidnesset said that Richard Smith had set up the trading house "forty years or more" earlier; Roger Williams testified that it occurred "forty-two years from this date" and acknowledged that Smith had built the "first English house" in the Narragansett country (see Bartlett's *Records of the Colony of Rhode Island*, 3:54-57). That would place Richard Smith at Cocumscussoc after July 1637 and before July 1639. John Greene (to distinguish him from John Greene, surgeon of Warwick) was one of Smith's agents who lived at the trading house and oversaw the business in Smith's absence. No documents link Richard Smith to the sale of slaves, and his 1664 will, a copy of which descended through the family, makes no mention of slaves. However, Richard Smith's full probate records have never been located, and an inventory of his personal estate, if ever discovered, would prove illuminating. John Wilcox, one of Richard Smith's trading rivals in Narragansett and New Amsterdam, was sued in Manhattan in a court case in June 1646 relating to the sale of an African woman (Dutch Manuscripts, IV:255), so the possibility that Smith participated in the same activity can't be ruled out. Slaves were brought into Rhode Island prior to 1652, when the colony passed a law limiting their servitude to ten years (Bartlett's *Records...*, 2:243); the law was generally ignored.

2. As published in J. Hammond Trumbull, *The True-blue laws of Connecticut and New Haven and the false blue-laws* ... (1876), 313. The last words of the paragraph are emphasized in the 1876 printed translation, suggesting they were also emphasized (underscored?) in the original document. However, a typewritten transcript of the Dutch manuscript and its translation by Arnold J.F. van Laer published in 1974 don't provide the emphasis, and van Laer translates the line as, "from which he shortly after died" (New York Historical Manuscripts: Dutch, IV:66).
3. OpDyck appears as witness to a deed at Cocumscussoc in June 1659 (Fones Record, 98); the inhabitants of Wickford are enumerated on 3 July 1663 (Fones Records, 24-25).
4. The sheriff's impropriety in marrying Newton to Joan Smith caused quite an uproar with the Dutch authorities, and one wonders if Newton colluded with or bribed the sheriff to expedite the marriage. The sheriff requested Richard Smith's permission to wed the couple, which Smith refused; the next day the sheriff married the couple anyway, secretly in his own home, and provided them "with bed and room to consummate the marriage" (see *New York Historical Manuscripts: Dutch*, IV:502-506). Newton's partner in the crime of adultery was a widow, Elizabeth Johnson, who while jailed bore their child named Benoni Newton. Roger Williams mentions Newton's plight in letters dated 16 Feb 1649/50 and 20 June 1650. In September 1651, Thomas Newton appears at Cocumscussoc as witness to Williams's sale of his trading house to Richard Smith (Fones Record, 93-94). Abigail (Newton) Updike's birth is unrecorded, but a Narragansett Church parish entry dated September 1726 gave her age as 63, putting her birth about 1663-64 (see Wilkins Updike, *A History of the Episcopal Church in Narragansett* ... (1908), III:411-412, Note 182.)
5. For more detail on Thomas Newton's connection with Barbados, see Clair Alonzo Newton, *History of the Newton Families of Colonial America* ... (1949), 10-17. A Thomas Newton does appear as a witness to wills made on Barbados in 1652 and 1654 (as well as 1670 and 1671), putting into question whether Thomas of Fairfield was in fact the one who wrote the letters in 1664-65 and the one who died in 1673 (See Joanne McRee Sanders, *Barbados Records: Wills, 1639-1725.* Vols. 1. (1979-1981). On the other hand, Thomas of Fairfield may have already been traveling to Barbados and making connections in the early 1650s after his retreat to Long Island.
6. A manuscript entitled *Recollections,* attributed to James Updike (1763-1855), is not dated but content suggests it was written before 1812 (RIHS MSS 770 Updike Papers).
7. Abigail Newton's passenger list is cited in John Camden Hotten, ed., *The Original Lists of Persons of Quality, Emigrants ... and Other Who Went from Great Britain to the American Plantations 1600-1700* (1874), 392. Clair Alonzo Newton speculates that Abigail went to Boston to live with her aunt, Elizabeth (Smith) Vial (*Newton Families,* 11). Vial had also inherited lands in Wickford from her father, Richard Smith. Abigail's witness of the Smith-Palmer land transaction is in the Fones Record, 157-159. No record

of the marriage of Lodowick Updike and Abigail Newton has been found, but their first child, Richard, was born about 1691.

8. Elder son James Smith may have remained in Manhattan with his younger brother Richard, but he died before 1660. Land records described in this discussion are compiled in I.N. Phelps Stokes, *The Iconography of Manhattan Island*, Vol. II (1916), 321–324; 405-406. The 1661 sale described a lot that bordered the "ho[use] and lot of R. Smith, Jr.," but since the younger Smith didn't actually own any property, the reference suggests he was living in the house at the time. The description and location of the company's slave quarters on Slyck Steegh are also in Stokes, 297-298.

9. The 1676 itemization is taken from a 1684 request by Richard Smith Jr for compensation from the United Colonies for items supplied to (or taken by) the garrison stationed at Smith's house during the Great Swamp campaign from December 1675 through April 1676. The numbers of Smith's livestock therefore were probably than greater than described (see *The Public Records of the Colony of Connecticut* (1859), 3:511-512). The 1692 count is from the inventory of Smith's estate after his death (RIHS MSS 770 Updike Papers). According to family lore, Joan Smith (wife of Richard Sr, mother of Richard Jr), brought from Gloucestershire her recipe for making cheese. She must have shared the process with her daughter-in-law, Esther, wife of Richard Jr, as Esther's presents of cheese are mentioned on several occasions in Smith's letters to Winthrop. In Rhode Island, the Smith's mixed breed of English and Dutch cattle eating Narragansett salt hay produced a hearty, salty cheese different than anything produced in Gloucestershire. The Smiths, family lore continues, shared the recipe with other farmers in the Narragansett country, and the cheese became a major export for the colony until the Revolutionary War. Called Narragansett or Rhode-Island cheese, it was shipped to the Caribbean and along the eastern seaboard; it was even advertised in Benjamin Franklin's Philadelphia newspaper. See Darrell McIntire, "Cheese-Making at Cocumscussoc," Cocumscussoc Association *Castle Chronicle*, 17:4 (Winter 2008) & 18:1 (Spring 2009).

10. See blog by Katherine Garland, Newport Historical Society, 17 Sep 2013 (http://www.spectacleoftoleration.org/african-spirituality-in-newport/)

11. For interpretation of Native American lithics at African-American archaeological sites, see Laura Wilkie, "Magic and Empowerment on the Plantation: An Archaeological Consideration of African-American World View," *Southeastern Archaeology*, 14:2 (Winter 1985), 142-146. For lithics at the Royall House, see Alexandra Chan, *Slavery in the Age of Reason: Archaeology at a New England Farm* (2007), 155-159.

12. Newport County Supreme Court, General Court of Trials, Vol. A (1671-1724), 496.

13. Few documents shed light on slavery in Lodowick Updike's household. Certainly from his uncle he had inherited Caesar and Sarah's five children, but whether he complied in giving them their freedom at age 30 is unknown. In North Kingstown records, Lodowick's fragmented will clearly names at least one slave, Penny, and the inventory of his personal

estate appears to repeat her name as "Penny Time." Others were likely mentioned in both documents but have been burned and obliterated from the manuscript. (Will of Lodowick Updike, made 1734, proved 22 March 1736/37. Town of North Kingstown, Rhode Island. Probate Records, 7:94-97; the inventory appears on 7:103-106.)

14. Wilkins Updike, *Memoirs of the Rhode Island Bar* (1842), 37.

15. "A New Map of the Island of Barbadoes," first drawn 1675-76, shows two adjoining Chace plantations on the coast near Bridgetown; the Newton plantation is in Christ Church (see John Carter Brown Archive of Early American Images, Record number 8189-32). John Chace married Ann Arnold, daughter of Benedict Arnold, in 1713; Daniel Updike married Sarah Arnold, Ann's sister, in 1716, and Sarah died in childbirth in 1718. (See *A History of the Episcopal Church in Narragansett ...* (1908), I:113, III:402-403, 418.)

16. Joseph Wanton (1705-1780) was the son of William Wanton (1673-1733), who successfully ran against Daniel Updike as governor of the colony in 1732 but died in office a year later. Joseph Wanton was a slave trader; in 1758 his ship, *King of Prussia*, was captured by privateers off the African coast with a cargo of 54 slaves. Like his father, Joseph too served as governor of the colony (1769-1775). He was Updike's stepson as follows: Joseph was the son of William Wanton's first wife, Ruth Bryant; William Wanton married second Mary Godfrey in 1717; about 1745, Daniel Updike married Wanton's widow, Mary (Godfrey) Wanton. She was Updike's third wife. (See "Edward Wanton" at http://minerdescent.com/2010/07/27/edward-wanton/)

17. For a description of Updike's professional career, see Catherine DeCesare, *Daniel Updike, General Attorney of the Colony of Rhode Island and Providence Plantations: An Archive Inventory* (2013).

18. Bartlett's *Records of the Colony of Rhode Island*, 4:330.

19. "An Inventory of the Personal Estate of Daniel Updike Esqr. of North Kingstown Deceased taken and Approved by us the Subscribers the 5th Day of June A.D. 1757" (RIHS MSS 770 Updike Papers). The subscribers, or inventory-takers, are not listed in this document. The header on this section indicates "18 Negroes," but 19 people are listed if the child with Lille is included (was Lille pregnant or was the child a newborn?). The valuation of the estate in today's money was calculated using the website "UK Inflation Calculator" (http://www.whatsthecost.com/cpi.aspx) and then converted from UK pounds to US dollars. By this calculation, Updike's total personal estate was worth $2.8 million in 2014. A higher value was derived using a similar tool from the Bank of England (http://www.bankofengland.co.uk/education/Pages/resources/inflationtools/calculator/index1.aspx). Real estate was not included in the probate. Given that he owned at least 3000 acres across three farms around Wickford, if not also property in Newport and elsewhere, Updike certainly ranked among the wealthiest inhabitants of the colony. The probate inventory also demonstrates that Updike shifted the farm away from the Smith model of cattle

for cheese production to sheep for wool and more particularly for meat (mutton), which was packed in butts (hence the need for cooper tools listed in the backroom) and shipped to Caribbean plantations. Updike's inventory lists only about 20 cattle but 270 sheep.

20. Daniel Goodwin, *A Letter Book and Abstract of Out Services Written during the Years 1743-1751 by the Revd. James MacSparran, doctor in Divinity, and sometime rector of Saint Paul's Church, Narragansett, Rhode Island* (1899), 15, 29.

21. Most notably by Joanne Pope Melish, *Disowning Slavery: Gradual Emancipation and "Race" in New England, 1780-1860* (2000), and Robert K. Fitts, *Inventing New England's Slave Paradise: Master/Slave Relations in Eighteenth-Century Narragansett, Rhode Island* (1998).

22. Louis E. Grivettie, et al., *Chocolate: history, culture, and heritage* (2009), 58-59. The original manuscript is in the Newport Historical Society, the Aaron Lopez Collection, Lopez Account Book 715:37.

23. As transcribed by Maureen Alice Taylor, *Runaways, Deserters, and Notorious Villains from Rhode Island Newspapers* (1998), I:2.

24. According to Robert K. Fitts, *Inventing New England's Slave Paradise: Master/Slave Relations in Eighteenth-Century Narragansett, Rhode Island* (1998), 118.

25. Daniel Updike (1761-1842), Day Book January – May 1791. Manuscript in Rhode Island Historical Society Library.

26. Although the 1800 census tallies two slaves, two years earlier an inventory of the Updike property in 1798 for the so-called "glass tax" listed only one slave, "One Negro woman have about Seventy Six years of age." [The Land and Houses of Lodowick Updike of North Kingston, December 12th, 1798. Updike Family Papers, Rhode Island Historical Society Manuscripts, Case 14:21-23.] By process of elimination I believe this woman to be the Lille listed in Daniel Updike's 1757 probate inventory.

27. 1790 Federal Census, North Kingston, Washington, R.I.; Roll M637_10, Page 84, Image 58. Births of the children appear in *Town of North Kingstown, Births Marriages,* 1:225, and are transcribed in James N. Arnold, *Vital Records of Rhode Island,* 5:107. In the census the word "Negro" is commonly appended for people of African descent. Also living in North Kingstown at the time was James Updike, the (white) grandson of Daniel Updike. Because James and Freelove named their first-born male Joseph, it is quite possible that James Updike, a child in Updike's household in 1757, was the son of the enslaved Joseph listed in the same document.

28. Ceasar and Christopher Updike are listed in Jay Coughtry, *The Notorious Triangle: Rhode Island and the African Slave Trade, 1700-1807*(1981). For background on African Americans as maritime workers, see Chris Odle, "Black Jacks: African American Mariners in Early America," The Freedom Trail Foundation (http://www.thefreedomtrail.org/educational-resources/article-black-jacks.shtml)

29. 1820 U S Census; Census Place: North Kingston, Washington, Rhode Island; Page: 94; NARA Roll: M33_115; Image: 98. 1830; Census Place: North Kingstown, Washington, Rhode Island; Series: M19; Roll: 167; Page: 173; Family History Library Film: 0022266. The date of the death of "Black James Updike" is recorded in the almanacs/diaries of Harris Smith (RIHS MSS 722).
30. For the General Assembly's law creating the Black Regiment, see Bartlett's *Records of the Colony of Rhode Island*, 8:358-363. For the Updikes' recruitment, see "A List of Slaves Enlisted in to the Continental Army. To whom belonged, with their value, in the year 1778, from Kings County," as published in *The Narragansett Historical Register*, I:4:313. For their service at Valley Forge, see Joseph Lee Boyle, *Death Seem'd to Stare: The New Hampshire and Rhode Island Regiments at Valley Forge* (2005), 164, as abstracted from National Archives Record Group 93, M246, "Revolutionary War Rolls, 1775-1783. This document gives earlier enlistment dates than the May 8 in the first source: March 3 for Moses and March 15 for Caesar.
31. All of the above provided by Cherry Fletcher Bamberg to the author in personal correspondence, 16 May 2011, citing the Revolutionary War Records, RIHS, Mss 673, sg 2, series 1, box 1, folder 41.
32. The pension claim is listed in June Clark Murtie, *The Pension Lists of 1792-1795* (1991), 151, citing the *American State Papers*, IX(1834):403. Caesar's account of work and payments appear in Daniel Updike (1761-1842), Day Book G (January 5, 1797 – February 23, 1798), 22 (Rhode Island Historical Society Manuscripts). Caesar is also listed in the manuscript index for the May 10, 1795 – June 14, 1796 daybook, but the entry is not found.
33. 1800 Federal Census, East Greenwich, Kent, R.I.; Roll: 45; Page: 73; Image: 146. 1810 Federal Census, North Kingstown, Washington, R.I.; Roll 59, Page 79, Image 162.
34. Copies of the application letters and supporting documents are in Revolutionary War Pension and Bounty-Land Warrant Application Files (NARA microfilm publication M804, roll 2435). Pension information is from United States Senate. Senate Document 514, Serial Nos. 249-51, Report from the Secretary of War, in Obedience to Resolutions of the Senate of the 5th and 30th of June, 1834, and the 3d of March, 1835, In Relation to the Pension Establishment of the United States. Washington, D.C.: Duff Green, 1835; as transcribed in The Pension Roll of 1835: Indexed Edition, 1992, I:801.
35. George Harris, "Ancient Burial Grounds of Old Kingstowne," c1883 manuscript in RIHS Library. This cemetery is catalogued as Rhode Island Historic Cemetery NK346. It contains only one marked grave: Tony, son of Tony Musnott and Amey Cole, d. May 10, 1764, 6 y, 4m. See Althea McAleer, et al., *Graveyards of North Kingstown, RI* (1992), 38.

Roll Call

FOOD FOR THOUGHT AS YOU LOOK
AT THE ROLL CALL SECTION

The lists which follow in this section are meant to be starting point for further research into the lives of the black residents of North Kingstown across the decades of the 1800s. In most cases, more information can be gleaned from checking the full record. The 1850, 1860, 1870, and 1880 censuses are available on line through various websites, both paid and free and I encourage you to examine them. It's very important to keep in mind that these censuses only include the black individuals and families counted, **not** all of them that lived in a community at the time of the census taking. Black people in the 1800s are among the most undercounted of all groups throughout census periods for a number of reasons having to do with both the mindsets of the census enumerators (takers) and the black individuals themselves. For these lists, I included all North Kingstown residents that fall into the following category designations; B- which stands for black, I – which stands for Indian, and Mu or M which stands for Mulatto/Mustee; two designations that indicate people of a mixed race heritage. For the most part these designations were made by the individual him or herself after being questioned by the enumerator; although some enumerators may have automatically placed light-skin blacks in the M/Mu category. The truth of the matter is that, in the case of nearly all South County RI blacks in that timeframe, the vast majority of individuals were of mixed race heritage of some form or another; an intriguing mix of West African blacks, Caribbean Blacks, Indigenous Native, and European/American white made up the heritage of these people. To further complicate this already complicated genealogy, recent studies have found that a majority of Caribbean blacks have a heritage that includes an ancestry that connects them back to the Narragansett and Wampanoag survivors of the King Phillip's War, who were forced into slavery on the Caribbean sugarcane plantations of the late 17th century.

A number of intriguing facts came to light in my mind as I made up these lists from the US census data. First and foremost it is clear to see that the pre-Civil War black population of North Kingstown, and through extrapolation all of South County, was predominantly made up of individuals that carried the surnames of a group of colonial era white families I call "The eleven". These families, the Smith/Updikes, Gardiners, Potters, Robinsons, Hazards, Watsons, Niles, Perrys, Browns, Babcocks, and Stantons make up the Narragansett Planters, a group of elite agribusinessmen of the period that operated large scale plantations in the same fashion that the southern cotton and tobacco plantation owners did, with slave labor. It's no coincidence that so many South

We Were Here Too

County black individuals share these names; their roots include the slaves of these people. Also interesting is the fact that so many of the additions to the region's post-Civil War black population came out of Virginia. It's also ponderously sad to see how early in life some of these children entered the work force. The thought of little 8 year old Ellen Berry working as a house servant in 1880 is tragic.

The listing of black mariners I have here has been gleaned from my own research into the topic as well as the work of my friend John F. Capron III, who self-published a wonderful resource book named *RI Mariners and Vessels – Who sailed from the Ports of East Greenwich & North Kingstown* utilizing research he did at the National Archives in Waltham, Massachusetts. If you have an interest in this topic, pick up John's work. This black mariners list is an ongoing work in progress and I expect to find more of these brave and hearty souls. It bears repeating that "at sea" was the one place where race truly did not matter; once the last line was cast off, men were judged solely by their abilities as sailors. Everyone on board put their lives in each other's hands, skin color didn't matter- coming home alive did. It must have been liberating for all of these men, a number of whom learned their trade as "slaves for hire" enriching the coffers of their owners who rented them out in the agricultural off-season.

Finally, the death list has been culled from the Vital Records of the Town of North Kingstown and cover the period of 1856 to 1909. Again if you have an interest in any of the folks listed here, I suggest you examine the full record as most often more information can be gleaned from them. As with the US Census data, these records only reflect reported deaths in North Kingstown **not** all deaths. White or Black, many folks in the period, especially those of meager means, just buried their dead and got on with their lives. Additional information can often be found in local church records.

1850 CENSUS

Bliss, James	18	laborer	Gardner, Jenny	65	servant
Bliss, Thomas	16	laborer	Gardner, James	60	laborer
Brown, James B.	39	laborer	Gardner, Abigail	46	keeping house
Brown, Catherine	34	housewife	Gardner, Stephen	28	whaleman
Brown, William	15		Gardner, Sarah	25	
Brown, Thomas E.	11		Gardner, Thomas	23	laborer
Brown, Ann E.	5		Gardner, William	20	miner
Brown, Alice	32		Gardner, Charles	18	laborer
Brown, William H.	5		Gardner, Ann	14	
Brown, John F.	3		Gardner, Alice	10	
Clinton, G. George	4		Gardner, Phebe	6	
Denby, Lucy	50		Gardner, Hannah F.	1	
Fry, Isabella	9	servant	Gardner, George	22	laborer
Gardner, Dorcas	55	housewife	Granderson, Edward	27	fisherman
Gardner, Thomas	43	mariner	Hazard, Henry A.	15	laborer

Name	Age	Occupation
Hazard, Margaret	62	housewife
Hazard, Benjamin	37	laborer
Hazard, Ann	38	housewife
Hazard, Benjamin Jr.	4	
Hazard, Charles H.	3	
Hazard, Willliam	1	
Hazard, Hannahritta	82	indian doctoress
Hill, Avery	24	laborer
Jones, Eliza	24	
Jones, Rosannah	6 mo	
Mcpharson, Henry	35	laborer
Mcpharson, Mary	40	housewife
Mcpharson, Isabella	15	
Mcpharson, Celia	7	
Mcpharson, Elizabeth	4	
Mcpharson, Charles	3	
Mcpharson, Eliza	1	
Nelson, John	9	
Onion, Thankful	60	servant
Peel, William	60	mariner
Peel, Fanny	58	housewife
Potter, Joseph G.	21	laborer
Robinson, Mary	50	
Robinson, Ceasar	88	none
Robinson, Lucy A.	11	
Robinson, William	36	laborer
Robinson, Susan	38	housewife
Robinson, Palmer	17	laborer
Robinson, Welcome	15	
Robinson, Gardiner	14	
Robinson, Ananias	12	
Robinson, Thomas	10	
Robinson, Nathaniel	8	
Robinson, James	5	
Robinson, Daniel	3	
Rodman, Timothy	42	laborer
Rodman, Sophia	52	housewife
Rodman, Isaac	14	
Rodman, Elizabeth	12	
Rodman, Aaron	88	laborer
Rodman, Harriet	35	servant
Roome, Sarah	57	
Roome, Elizabeth	34	
Roome, Mary	23	
Roome, Jane	22	
Roome, William H.	18	laborer
Roome, James	14	
Roome, John	6	
Roome, Huldah A.	2	
Roome, William	52	laborer
Roome, Patience	50	housewife
Roome, Nathaniel	48	laborer
Roome, Deborah	44	housewife
Roome, George R.	15	
Roome, Hannah F.	11	
Roome, Ellen M.	4	
Thomas, Richard	42	laborer
Thomas, Rachel	40	housewife
Thomas, John	26	laborer
Thomas, Lucy	21	housewife
Thomas, Harriet	1	
Thomas, Braddock	28	laborer
Thomas, Nancy	34	housewife
Thomas, Abby F.	11	
Thomas, Michael H.	9	
Thomas, Isabel	7	
Thomas, Susan	20	servant
Watson, Richard	46	laborer
Watson, Memby	41	housewife
Watson, Daniel	22	laborer
Watson, Elizabeth	18	
Watson, Maryjane	15	
Watson, Richard	13	
Watson, James	11	
Watson, Abby	6	
Weeden, Samuel	27	laborer
Weeden, Eliza	30	housewife
Weeden, Mary C.	12	
Weeden, John F.	7	
Weeden, James	4	
Weeden, Elizabeth N.	5	
Weeden, Edward A.	3	
Weeden, Samuel Jr.	6 mo	
Weeden, Joseph R.	24	laborer
Weeden, Margaret	38	
Weeden, Susan	23	servant
Weeden, John	20	laborer
Williams, John	37	cook

1860 CENSUS

Bliss, James	30	farmhand	Robinson, Susan	16	
Browning, Content	54	housewife	Robinson, Salana	22	housewife
Browning, Nancy	66	housewife	Rooms, Deborah	50	housewife
Browning, Daniel G.	27	farmhand	Rooms, William	63	laborer
Dyer, Sarah	26	?	Rooms, Patience	59	housewife
Gardiner, Adam	47	farmhand	Rooms, Ellen	14	
Grandson, Betsy	27	housewife	Sambo, Hannah	20	servant
Grandson, Daniel	9		Sharp, Cebastus	16	farmhand
Grandson, Charles	4		Taylor, James	14	farmhand
Hazard, Benjamin	40	farmhand	Taylor, John	62	farmhand
Hazard, Henry A.	26	mariner	Taylor, Warren	8	
Hazard, Mary C.	21	housewife	Taylor, George	5	
Hazard, Nancy	22	?	Taylor, Ann	50	housewife
Hazard, James	4		Taylor, John Jr.	24	farmhand
Hazard, Anna	2		Taylor, Lyman	12	farmhand
Hazard, Ann	44	housewife	Thomas, Harriet	11	housemaid
Hazard, Anthony B.	14	farmhand	Thomas, Richard	46	fishmonger
Hazard, Charles	11		Thomas, Nancy	45	housewife
Hazard, William	10		Thomas, Henry M.	20	?
Hazard, Lucy A.	8		Thomas, Rachel	48	
Hazard, Margaret E.	3		Wamsley, Sarah	79	poorfarm
Hull, Susan F.	7		Watson, Thomas B.	14	
Laforcet, Edward	30	farmhand	Watson, Ann	38	?
Lippitt, Aaron	70		Weeden, Isabella	70	
Lippitt, George	24	laborer	Weeden, John T.	16	farmhand
Lippitt, Elizabeth	22	housewife	Weeden, John N.	18	mariner
Lippitt, Betsy	60	housewife	Weeden, Lucy	18	servant
Mcpharson, Henry	50	laborer	Weeden, William	44	farmhand
Mcpharson, Charles	15	laborer	Weeden, Hannah	38	housewife
Mcpharson, John	7		Weeden, Charles	20	farmhand
Mcpharson, Mary	47	housewife	Weeden, York	16	farmhand
Mcpharson, Eliza	12		Weeden, William Jr.	13	
Peel, William	60	mariner	Weeden, James	10	
Peel, Lucy	55	housewife	Weeden, Mary	5	
Potter, Joseph G.	31	factoryhand	Weeden, Samuel	2	
Potter, Hannah	21	housewife	Weeden, Elizabeth N.	15	
Potter, Laura	3		Weeden, James	13	
Potter, Ida	1		Weeden, Edward E.	11	
Robinson, Anna	22	housewife	Weeden, Margaret A.	10	
Robinson, Gardiner	24	farmhand	Weeden, Samuel	8	
Robinson, Harriet	23	farmhand	Weeden, William	7	
Robinson, Mary	59	washerwoman	Weeden, Abby	4	
Robinson, Lucy	3		Weeden, Braddock	2	

Weeden, Harriet   1
Weeks, Uriah   39 barber
Weeks, Sarah   29 housewife

Weeks, William   4
Weeks, Ida   1

1870 CENSUS

Artibee, Mary	27	servant	Perry, James C.	7	
Bliss, James U.	39	farmhand	Perry, Amelia	2	
Boat, Nathaniel	30	laborer	Perry, Javis	4 mos.	
Bradford, Louise	30	?	Potter, Joseph G.	41	laborer
Chase, James A.	30	teamster	Potter, Hannah	31	housewife
Gardiner, Adam	60	farmhand	Potter, Laura	13	?
Garnett, Ann	65	servant	Potter, Ida	11	
Granderson, Edwin	43	laborer	Potter, Walter S.	10	
Granderson, Betsey	38	housewife	Potter, Herbert J.	7	
Granderson, Daniel	19	?	Potter, Frederick	3	
Granderson, Etta	20	servant	Potter, Arthur	1	
Granderson, Charles	13	?	Robinson, Annier	35	laborer
Granderson, George H. L.	2		Robinson, Mary	69	housewife
Hazard, Benezet	55	farmhand	Robinson, Prince	51	laborer
Hazard, Benjamin	23	laborer	Robinson, Sarah A.	48	housewife
Hazard, Henry A.	30	mariner	Robinson, Mary A.	19	?
Hazard, Margaret	14	servant	Robinson, William F.	22	laborer
Hazard, Sarah E.	20	housewife	Robinson, Esther E.	16	?
Hazard, Charles	20	laborer	Robinson, Benjamin G.	14	farmhand
Hazard, William	18	laborer	Robinson, Hannah	18	?
Hazard, Maggie	16	servant	Rose, James	25	groomsman
Hazard, Nancy	23	housewife	Sheffield, William	24	farmhand
Hazard, James H.	13	school	Smart, Mary	13	servant
Hazard, Anna E.	11		Smith, Mary	23	servant
Hazard, Ardelia	2		Sweet, Ophelia	60	servant
Hines, Caroline	15	servant	Taylor, Prince A.	27	laborer
Holden, Fannie E.	11	servant	Taylor, Lorraine	27	housewife
Jenkins, Mattie	19	servant	Taylor, Lilia	7	
Mcpharson, Henry	69	laborer	Taylor, Henry	3	
Mcpharson, Mary	57	housewife	Thomas, Nancy	50	servant
Onion, Thankful	80	servant	Thomas, Richard	53	fishmonger
Parkill, Cornelia	6		Thomas, Michael H.	20	mariner
Peel, Lucy	63	housewife	Thomas, Rachel	58	housewife
Perry, Amey	19	servant	Watson, Robbin	65	laborer
Perry, Ceasar	41	laborer	Watson, Patience	69	housewife
Perry, Mary A.	37	housewife	Weeden, Alfred	15	farmhand
Perry, George H.	15	?	Weeden, Hannah	45	servant
Perry, Harriet G.	14	?	Weeden, Ida F.	19	servant
Perry, Alfred C. A.	9		Weeden, Mellisa	15	servant

Weeden, William	55	laborer	Weeden, Charles H.	5	
Weeden, Hannah	50	housewife	Weeden, Anna E.	1	
Weeden, Lucy	27	servant	Weeks, Uriah	48	barber
Weeden, George W.	19	laborer	Weeks, Sarah	40	housewife
Weeden, James P.	19	laborer	Weeks, Ida	11	
Weeden, William	24	laborer	Weeks, Frank D.	9	
Weeden, Mary F.	15	housekeeper	Weeks, Arthur M.	5	
Weeden, Samuel L.	11		White, Christiana	25	servant
Weeden, Abby F. J.	7				

1880 CENSUS

Artist, Lucy	30	housewife	Price, Robert L.	21	farmhand
Artist, Thomas	35	laborer	Reynolds, Mary J.	28	housewife
Berry, Ellen	8	servant	Reynolds, William	49	farmhand
Boon, Emeline	70	servant	Reynolds, William Jr.	2	
Chase, Christina	30	housewife	Romes, Claire	3	
Chase, James	35	teamster	Romes, Ella	21	servant
Chase, Mary A.	4		Smart, Josephine	21	servant
Chase, William H.	7		Taylor, Hannah L.	19	servant
Gladding, Walter	16	servant	Thomas, Joseph	27	farmhand
Granderson, Charles E.	24	farmhand	Thomas, Nancy	70	washerwoman
Granderson, Edward L.	53	farmhand	Thomas, Rachel	67	housewife
Granderson, Elizabeth	48	housewife	Thomas, Richard	69	fishpeddler
Granderson, George L.	11	student	Waddy, Cornelius	24	servant
Granderson, Mary E.	18	washerwoman	Watson, Ann	60	housewife
Hazard, Augustus	49	fisherman	Watson, Ruthanne	80	
Hazard, Frederick A.	13	student	Weeden, Abby F.	19	housekeeper
Hazard, James H.	21	farmhand	Weeden, Charles H.	42	farmhand
Hazard, Lavina	1		Weeden, Eliza	65	washerwoman
Hazard, Nancy	38	housewife	Weeden, George E.	25	laborer
Huff, Bartley	27	farmhand	Weeden, George E. Jr.	1 mo.	
Jourden, Andrew	7		Weeden, Hannah	50	housewife
Jourden, Fred	9		Weeden, Ida F.	25	housekeeper
Jourden, Isabella	4		Weeden, James K. P.	25	laborer
Mcpharson, Abby	23	housewife	Weeden, Mary A.	23	?
Mcpharson, Alonzo	9		Weeden, Samuel	22	laborer
Mcpharson, Charity	1		Weeden, Sarah E.	19	housekeeper
Mcpharson, John	28	farmhand	Weeden, William R.	60	farmer
Mcpharson, Charles	34	farmhand	Weeden, William R. Jr.	36	farmhand
Mcpharson, Mary G.	6 mo		Weeden, Lillian B.	17	servant
Price, Charles	16	farmhand	White, Cornelia	16	student
Price, Henrietta	35	washerwoman	Wilson, George H.	30	coachman
Price, John H.	40	farmhand	Wilson, Lucy A.	32	washerwoman

RECORDED DEATHS   1856-1909

NAME	DOD	AGE	OCCUPATION
Adams, Mildred	1900	3	
Adams, Athena	1900	1	
Adams, Lewis	1900	1	
Albert (?), Phyllis	1859	70	
Artist, Lucy	1908	59	housekeeper
Berry, Frank	1879	30	hosteler
Berry, Margaret	1888	80	
Bird, George H.	1873	1	
Brown, Elmira	1884	64	
Browning, Content	1860	55	
Browning, Nancy	1866	77	
Bryant, Joseph	1906	53	Farmer
Dailey, Mary	1909	74	
Gardiner, Benjamin C.	1864	29	Soldier
Gardiner, Adam	1876	62	Laborer
Gardner, Nathaniel	1858	58	Mariner
Granderson, Nicholas	1859	1	
Granderson, Abraham L.	1865	2	
Granderson, Julia	1874	2 mos.	
Granderson, Edward L.	1885	61	Laborer
Hazard, Ann	1868	55	
Hazard, Henry A.	1897	60	Laborer
Hyles, Harriet	1867	60	
Jordan, Harold	1904	2	
Lippitt, William	1862	20	Sailor
Lippius, Caroline	1890	72	
Mawney, Catherine	1856	62	
Mcpherson, Eliza	1865	16	
Mcpherson, Henry	12/10/1873	74	
Onion, Thankful	1881	95	
Peel, Lucy	1871	75	
Perry, Nelly	1866	1	
Perry, Abram	1873	73	Laborer
Perry, Cornelia	1904	24	
Price, Henrietta	1887	46	
Price, Ida	1893	4	
Price, William	1900	2	
Price, John	1903	67	Farmer
Real, Jane	1893	42	Housekeeper
Robinson, Mary	1872	72	
Robinson, Addie Bell	1884	1	
Roome, James	1864	27	Soldier

PARENTS	OTHER
George & Angeline Adams	
George & Angeline Adams	
George & Angeline Adams	
John Sheffield	
Samuel & Margaret Berry	
? Garrett	
Samuel & Celia Bird	
Edward A. & Phela Ann Brown	
	Murdered
Primus Browning	
Joseph & Francis Bryant	
Samuel & Maria Dailey	
	Malaria -Fort Jackson LA
Jenny Gardiner	
Edward & Betsey Granderson	
Edward & Betsey Granderson	
Edward & Betsey Granderson	Consumption
Abraham & Deborah Granderson	
Peter & Lucy Weeden	Consumption
Betsey Weeden	
William & Flora Jordan	
Aaron & Betsey Lippitt	Intemperence
Edward A. & Phela Ann Brown	Consumption
Jack Ayrault/Phillis Tillinghast	
Henry & Mary Mcpherson	Consumption
Gardiner & Celia Mcpherson	Born a slave in Washington DC
James & Magaret Garrett	
Caesar & Mary Perry	
Caesar Perry	
Thomas & Almira Potter	Pregnancy complications
William & Harriet Lincoln	
John & Susan Price	
John & Susan Price	
Sam Price	
John & Ann Taylor	
Nancy Hall	
	Malaria -Fort Jackson LA

NAME	DOD	AGE	OCCUPATION
Sampson, Nellie	1907	33	
Taylor, Fanny	1878	29	
Taylor, John	1892	56	Laborer
Thomas, Braddock	1858		Fisherman
Thomas, Rachel	1884	75	
Thomas, Richard	1890	83	
Waite, George S. Jr.	1873	2	
Walmsley, Sarah	1860	92	
Watson, Memby	1859	55	
Watson, John	1865	14	
Watson, Richard	1867	63	Laborer
Watson, Patience	1873	84	
Watson, Ann	1881	72	
Watson, Amy	1883	92	
Weeden, Joseph	1857	28	Laborer
Weeden, Baby	1857	3 mos.	
Weeden, Samuel	1858		Fisherman
Weeden, Charles H. W.	1863	24	Soldier
Weeden, York	1872	29	Laborer
Weeden, Lucy Ann	1875	32	washerwoman
Weeden, Eunice	1879	48	
Weeden, Hannah	1879	45	
Weeden, William R.	1888	74	laborer
Weeks, William	1862	7	

PARENTS	OTHER
William & Rosanna Fry	
Elizabeth Cole	
John & Ann Taylor	
	Drowned
Rachel Smith	
Isabella Thomas	
George S. & Abby Waite	
Samson & Abigail Gardner	
	Consumption
Caleb & Sylvia Watson	
Caesar & Hannah Perry	Burned
Cudjoe Gardner	
Sarah Robinson	
Peter & Isabella Weeden	
Samuel & Eliza Weeden	
	Drowned
William R. & Hannah Weeden	Dropsy
William R. & Hannah Weeden	
William R. & Hannah Weeden	
John & Sarah Taylor	
York & Deborah (Case)Weeden	
York & Deborah (Case)Weeden	
Uriah & Sarah Weeks	Drowned

BLACK MARINERS OF NORTH KINGSTOWN, 1790-1880

Bradfield, Echo
Bunday, Peter
Clifford, William
Daley, Amos
Francis, John
Gardner, Isaac
Gardner, Josiah
Gardner, Silas
Gardner, Peter
Gardner, Winsor
Gardner, Cyrus

Gardner, Richard
Gardner, Amos
Gardner, Thomas
Gardner, Stephen
Hall, Amos
Hazard, Henry A.
Helme, James
Lewis, John
Mcpherson, Henry
Onion, Nathaniel
Peel, William

Rose, Caesar
Sambo, Samuel
Sambo, William
Smith, Domini
Taylor, James
Thomas, Michael H.
Updike, Christopher
Updike, Caesar
Weeden, John
Williams, Frederick
Williams, John

Index

Made in the USA
Middletown, DE
01 March 2015